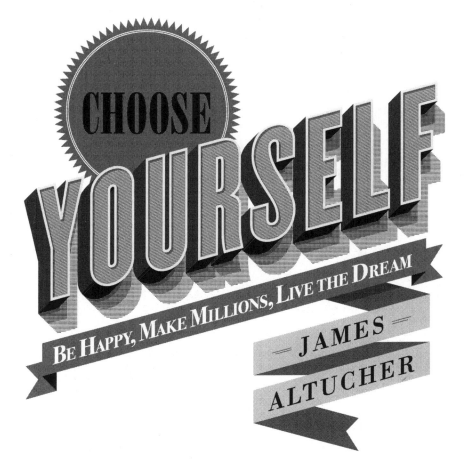

CHOOSE YOURSELF

BE HAPPY, MAKE MILLIONS, LIVE THE DREAM

JAMES

ALTUCHER

LIONCREST
PUBLISHING

Library of Congress Control Number: 2013940716

ISBN: 978-1-4903-1337-5

Printed in the United States of America

Cover design by: Herb Thornby
Interior design by: 1106 Design

Here's the Deal

I don't need to make a dime off of this book. The ideas in the book have already made me wealthy in many ways. What I really care about is that as many people as possible read this book and understand this message, even if it puts my own personal investment at risk.

Here's how I'm going to try and create a situation where as many people as possible get this message:

I know nobody values books—or anything—that are given away for free. So, I'm not going to do that. This isn't one of those ineffectual self-help books designed to look good on your shelf. You either read the book and use these ideas, or you shouldn't bother. That's why you have to front the purchase price. *But,* if you can prove to me that you have actually read the book, I will give you your money back. It's an investment that's all upside on your part.

How do you prove to me you've read the book? Do the following:

Within the first three months of the official publication date, do these two things:

1) **Send me a copy of the receipt to IReadChooseYourself@ gmail.com.** There is a kindle version, a hardcover, and an audio version and they all cost different amounts. I need to know what you paid.

2) **Then choose one of the following to send together with the receipt:**

    - *You can write an honest review* on Amazon or GoodReads or your blog.

    - *You can take a photograph* of yourself reading the book.

    - *You can write me a testimonial or an e-mail* asking me questions that show you've read the book.

If you can think of other ways, that's fine too. The point is: prove to me you read the book, and get your money back. Or, you can tell me to give it to a charity. This is the charity I will give it to:

WomenForWomen International

I'm a man of my word. If every single person who buys the book takes advantage of this opportunity, then I will make zero on it. But I'll be just as happy because it means the message will spread and you, the people who read the book, will be helped.

I know I was helped. This book has worked for me. I chose myself.

"Altucher has turned his misfortune into a source of wisdom and comfort for the despondent."
(BUSINESS WEEK)

"James Altucher is scary smart"
(STEVEN DUBNER, AUTHOR OF FREAKONOMICS)

"James Altucher is the best blogger of our generation."
(TIMOTHY SYKES, THE REBEL MILLIONAIRE)

"We are beginning to build a massive amount of respect for James Altucher due to his willingness to say things that will get him absolutely pilloried by the masses."
(BUSINESS INSIDER)

"James is one of the most successful and content people I know."
(MACHAEL LAZEROW, FOUNDER OF BUDDY MEDIA AND GOLF.COM)

"If you need to see an example of vulnerability done well, just read the work of James Altucher."
(SEARCH ENGINE JOURNAL)

DEDICATION

I Choose Myself!

TABLE OF CONTENTS

FOREWORD

I started out as a computer science major. I then got excited about improvisational comedy. I then somehow ended up as CEO of Twitter. We live in a world where the yellow brick road has many forks and can take us on many incredible journeys.

It's increasingly difficult to know the final destination of these journeys.

The day and age of the massive corporations that take care of us from beginning to end are over. But that is exciting news. It means we can choose the life we want for ourselves. You choose that life by doing the best you can right in this moment. Right now. By being bold in this moment. Right now. There is no other moment to wait for. Twitter is about the entire world conversation right in this moment. It's the improvisation, right now, of the planet. And yes, it's often comedy. And it's often about people reinventing themselves and starting new conversations for their lives.

What I like about James and his book is you can tell he came from a similar roller coaster. He chose his own path to success without knowing the outcome. And what happens to him later--well, hopefully he won't end up in a gutter. Who knows?

The key is to be bold right in this moment. As James says in the title of this book, "Choose Yourself," and he explains how. Choose yourself right now.

If you do this, not only can you not plan the impact you're going to have, you often won't recognize it while you're having it. But one thing is for sure: if you don't make courageous choices for yourself, nobody else will.

There's no one path. There's every path. Every path starts with this one moment. Did you choose yourself for this moment? Can you be bold? Then all paths will lead to the same place. Right now.

#chooseyourself

— Dick Costolo, CEO of Twitter

I Chose Myself:
An Introduction

I was going to die. The market had crashed. The Internet had crashed. Nobody would return my calls. I had no friends. Either I would have a heart attack or I would simply kill myself. I had a $4 million life insurance policy. I wanted my kids to have a good life. I figured the only way that could happen was if I killed myself. My expenses were out of control. I'd made some money and amped up my lifestyle to drunken-rock-star status. Then I promptly lost it, my bank account bumping along zero during the worst economy in maybe twenty years. I'm talking about 2002, but I could also have been talking about 2008: the year I lost my home, my family, my friends, money, jobs.

The excruciating downward spiral began in 1998 when I sold a company right as the dot-com bubble was really starting to swell. I was one of the smart ones, I thought. I was cashing out. Then I did everything wrong. I bought a house I couldn't afford. I had expensive habits I couldn't maintain. I gambled, and

1

squandered, and gave, and lent to everyone I knew. Hundreds of thousands of dollars. Then millions of dollars.

I started another company. I put millions into that. I felt like I needed to buy love. And if I didn't have an enormous amount of money to buy it, nobody would love me. That failed.

I lost my house. I lost all my money. I lost any self-esteem I had. I lost my friends. I had no idea what I was going to do. I failed at every attempt to right the ship, to succeed.

I would look at my daughters and cry because I felt like I had ruined their lives. I wasn't just a personal failure, or a failure in business, I was a failure as a father, as well. I didn't even have enough money every month to pay the mortgage that kept the roof over their heads.

I was officially lost. I had nothing left. Zero. *Less* than zero, actually, because I had debts. Millions in debts.

By 2002 there was nothing left in the ATM machine. I thought running out of money would be my worst moment. Worse than death. I was wrong.

At the end of 2002 I had a conversation with my parents. I was angry and depressed. We got into an argument. Over what—it doesn't matter anymore.

I hung up the phone and cut them off.

Over the next several months my father tried to reach out to me. I was starting to come back. I was writing. I was appearing on TV. He congratulated me. His final congratulations were about six months after I last spoke to him.

I didn't respond.

A week later he had a stroke. He never spoke again. He died without me ever speaking to him again.

And I was still broke, hungry, despairing, and depressed. I was in a constant state of panic. Nobody was helping me.

I Chose Myself: An Introduction

Nobody was giving me any chances. Nobody was giving me an outlet to prove how talented I was. I knew I had to hustle to make it, but the world was upside down and I didn't know how to straighten things out. To make things right.

For all intents and purposes, 2008 was a carbon copy of 2002. I managed to get myself back on my feet. I built and sold another company. I made a lot of money and then, through mindless squandering, I pissed it all away. Again. Except this time I was getting a divorce, losing even more friends, failing at two other companies at the same time, and I had no clue what I was going to do to climb out of the hole I'd dug for myself.

This kind of thing hasn't just happened to me once. Or twice. But many times. In the past twenty years I've failed at about eighteen of the twenty businesses I've started. I've probably switched careers five or six times in various sectors ranging from software to finance to media. I've written ten books. I've lost multiple jobs. I've been crushed, on the floor, suicidal, desperate, anxious, depressed. And each time, I've had to reinvent myself, reinvent my goals and my career. On most occasions, I didn't realize what steps I was repeating over and over, both positive and negative. Once I achieved success I would inevitably return to my negative habits and start squandering my good fortune.

Something about this last time in 2008 was different, though. The world was changing. Money was leaving the system. Everyone was getting fired. It felt like the opportunities were disappearing as fast as the money. Now it wasn't just me who was failing, it was the entire world, and there was no way out.

My stomach hurt all day thinking about it. *There is no way out. There is no way out.* I kept repeating it in my head. I felt like I could will myself to death with those words. But I couldn't. I had kids. I had to get better. *I had to.* I had to take care of myself. To take care of my children. I had to figure out, once and for all, how to get out of the hole, how to get off the floor, and stay there. I had to figure out, from the inside out, what was going to transform me into someone who would not just succeed, but thrive.

That's when it clicked. When everything changed. When I realized that nobody else was going to do it for me. If I was going to thrive, to survive, I had to choose myself. In every way. The stakes have risen too high not to.

We can no longer afford to rely on others and repeat the same mistakes from our pasts. The tide has come in and with it has come dramatic change to the landscape of our lives. As we will see in the next few chapters, the middle class has caved in, jobs are disappearing and every industry is in the process of transformation. In order to keep up, individuals have to transform also.

That means every second, you have to choose yourself to succeed. For me, I had to look back at my life and figure out (finally!) what I did every time I got off the floor, dusted myself off, went back out there and did it again. Because now there is no room to fall back down. I used to knock on wood every morning, literally and figuratively, praying I didn't fall back into my addictive behaviors. Choosing myself has changed that thought process.

Now, every day when I wake up I am grateful. I have to be. And I have to count the things that are abundant in my life. Literally count them. If I don't they will begin to disappear. I've watched them disappear before. I don't want it to happen again.

In some cultures, like Buddhism, you *want* things in your life to disappear, to reduce your needs and desires. To achieve some form of enlightenment. I believe in this brand of spirituality as well. I don't think it and abundance are mutually exclusive at all. If you lower your expectations, for instance, your expectations are easy to exceed.

Plus—and I hate to say it—first you have to pay the bills. The bills are expensive. And it's getting harder to find the opportunities to pay those bills. It's one thing to know "The Secret" or take whatever life-affirming steps you've read about in order to bring positivity into your life, but it's something else altogether to actually create opportunities for yourself.

You're definitely not going to find them reading a book. It's a moment by moment effort in your daily life. It's a practice that interweaves health with the tools of financial experts and a macro-level understanding of this economic shitstorm we find ourselves in today.

In the past four years I've begun writing about this practice and the steps I took on my journey back from the grave. In the process, my life has changed so much for the positive it's like magic. It's beyond magic, because I never would have dreamed this was possible. I've made millions in various businesses and investments (and not lost or squandered them), I've met and married the love of my life, I've gotten in shape, and every day I wake up and do exactly what I want to do. Not only have I seen the results for myself, I've seen them for countless of my readers who successfully applied the same principles I applied to my own life.

I write about it in this book. I chose myself. And you will also.

THE ECONOMIC HISTORY OF
THE CHOOSE YOURSELF ERA

F or the past five thousand years, people have been largely
enslaved by a few select masters who understood how violence,
religion, communication, debt, and class warfare all work
together to subjugate a large group of people.

The Gutenberg printing press was the first crack in the
prison. It allowed people to start breaking out of their solitary
confinement cells by spreading ideas across large distances, and
allowing those ideas to mate with one another. This resulted
first in the Renaissance, then the Protestant Reformation, and
ultimately enough discoveries in science to ignite the Industrial
Revolution.

But the Choose Yourself era had its direct roots in World
War II. And basically, women brought it on.

In World War II, 16 million American men left the United
States in order to kill people. Meanwhile, someone needed to
work the factories and offices to keep the country running.
Women stepped in and filled the task.

When the men came back, the women, quite correctly, realized that they didn't want to just stay at home anymore. They wanted to work and contribute and make money. Making money was fun and it gave them independence.

Suddenly, we went from having single-income families to two-income families in a booming postwar economy.

For the first time in about thirty years, Americans had money. A lot of it. And American industrialization was spreading throughout the world. Before long the US controlled the global economy. Global conglomerates rose from the ashes of near-bankrupt companies that barely survived the Great Depression.

For the first time in decades, Americans didn't have to worry about losing their jobs. There were plenty of jobs and men and women to fill them. The rise of the double-income family brought more money into every house.

What did everyone do with the money? They bought the so-called American Dream. A dream that was never thought of by the founders of the United States but became so ingrained in our culture starting in the 1950s that to dispute it would be almost as anti-American as disputing the wisdom of the US Constitution.

What was the American Dream?

It started with the house and the white picket fence. People didn't have to live in cities anymore. In apartments with people on top of them, on either side of them. When our grandparents were growing up most people lived in apartment buildings. The building shared a clothesline, all the kids played in the fire hydrant right out front, you could hear a fart three doors down. The smell of sewage and the constant battles with bed bugs were a normal part of life for tens of millions of immigrants.

My parents. Your parents.

Now it was different. They could move to the suburbs, with wide-open streets and neighborhood swimming pools and brightly-colored strip malls. They could have a yard. SPACE! Then they bought a car that they drove to work on the huge 4-lane highways. Then the second car for the summer road trips.

And then magic! A TV to keep them entertained during the now-quiet suburban nights. Then a color TV! *Captain Kirk and Lieutenant Uhuru kissing in color!* And if you had extra money after that, you sent your kids to colleges that were springing up all over the country so they could get even better jobs and make more money and have bigger houses.

You might think I'm using the phrase "American Dream" because that's just the general expression people use to describe the white-picket fence mythology.

I wish that were the case.

In fact, "the American Dream" comes from a marketing campaign developed by Fannie Mae to convince Americans newly flush with cash to start taking mortgages. Why buy a home with your own hard-earned money when you can use somebody else's? It may be the best marketing slogan ever conceived. It was like a vacuum cleaner that sucked everyone into believing that a $15 trillion mortgage industry would lead to universal happiness. "The American Dream" quickly replaced the peace and quiet of the suburbs with the desperate need to always stay ahead.

For our entire lives, we have been fooled by marketing slogans and the Masters of the Universe who created them. I don't say this in an evil way. I don't blame them. I never blame anyone but myself. Every second I am manipulated and coerced and beaten down it's because I've allowed it. They were just doing their jobs. But still…they are the manipulators. Now we have to learn how to discern the foolish from the wise and build our own lives.

There's a saying, "The learned man aims for more. But the wise man decreases. And then decreases again."

Everyone was learned. And they wanted two cars instead of one. A bigger house. Every kid in college. A bigger TV. How could we keep paying for that? Double incomes were no longer enough!

The 1960s fueled the wealth engine with a stock market boom. And then "The Great Society." A new marketing slogan! When the stock market stalled, the 1970s introduced massive inflation in order to keep people's incomes going up. The term "Keeping up with the Joneses" was introduced into popular culture in 1976 to refer to the idea that we are never satisfied anymore. No matter how many material goods we accumulate, there's always the mysterious "Jones family" who has more. So *we* need more.

In the 1980s we again had a stock market boom. And when that leveled off, we had the junk bond debt boom to keep Americans flush in cash. The '90s brought us both the "peace dividend" from the downfall of the Soviet Bloc and the Internet boom. Even when Asia crashed, Alan Greenspan, the Federal Reserve chairman, kept the party going by artificially pumping money into the system—not only to stave off the effects of a potential "Asian Contagion" but out of fear that the show would be over if Y2K shut off all the lights.

The party had to continue! Despite the fact that median earnings for male workers had been going down since 1970 and it was only going to get worse. Don't believe me? Believe the data:

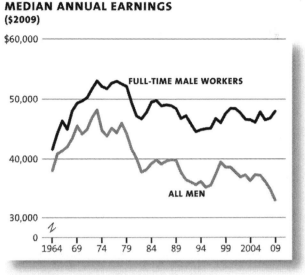

MEDIAN ANNUAL EARNINGS
($2009)

NOTE: Men Ages 25-64. Adjusted for inflation using CPI-U.
SOURCE: "The Problem With Men: A Look at Long-Term Employment Trends,"
The Hamilton Project, December 2010. (http://www.brookings.edu/opinions/
2010/1203_jobs_greenstone_looney.aspx)

Every economist in the world can try to explain away this graph, but its downward thrust was inexorable for the reasons I will describe throughout this book: among them increasing efficiencies, globalization, technological innovation, and the fact that your bosses simply hate you.

That's right, they hate you. You created more and more value. They paid you less and less. That's the definition of "disdain" in my book.

And it's not just your boss. He's just trying to survive also. It's his boss. And then the boss of that boss. All the way up the food chain. And who is at the top? We will never know. Trust me, you and I will never know who is at the top. I don't say this to be conspiratorial. It's just a fact.

Then the Internet crashed. And instead of shoring up the foundations of the American economy, Alan Greenspan kept the Federal Reserve's foot on the pedal and pressed it to the floor, printing money that flooded into the housing system. Housing prices tripled in many parts of the country, creating artificial prosperity that sent U.S. wealth to its highest point ever.

Of course consumer spending increased right along with it, thanks to the banks. They allowed people to use their home equity to back their credit cards. Can you imagine? Every vacation you took and put on your VISA was paid for by the flimsy walls of the house that kept your kids warm at night. A house that was falling apart around you—like your life—because you couldn't afford to repair it because VEGAS BABY, VEGAS!

Credit card debt went from $700 billion in 2005 to $2.5 TRILLION in 2007. Two short years. Now everybody had wide screen TVs, two houses, the latest Viking kitchen equipment, a boat, two environmentally sustainable cars (to assuage the guilt for their voracious consumption), and ate out two or three times a week.

And when I say "everybody", what I really mean is "me". I don't know anything about everybody. I only know what happened to me. And I was up to my neck in it.

After starting many companies, making and losing millions, thinking for once I might have "made it," I had to ask myself: what was "IT"? What did I truly "make"? I can't even think about it. Every time I do, I start scratching big scabs off my back like a tweaker or a schizophrenic. It's like I develop an acute spontaneous nervous condition. My hands shake and stutter because...

Argh!

2008.

The tide came in. Everyone was suddenly naked! We all know what happened: everything crashed. In prior economic boom/busts, America's technological innovation has somewhat buffered the middle class. But that period is over. There are no more booms on the horizon that we can latch onto. The smartest graduate students in China, India, and elsewhere are staying home. And the ones who come to the United States to study are going back after graduation instead of moving to Silicon Valley and starting companies and creating jobs and wealth. The companies and people in the United States who are greatly increasing in wealth are those who invest overseas in search of cheaper capital per technological development.

The only thing left was just the government increasing its debt. The government saved every bank *and* started paying interest to the banks on all their assets, artificially keeping the entire financial system healthy. Let me put this in a little more perspective.

Prices are always going to go up. The reason is simple: deflation is scarier than inflation. In a deflationary environment, people stop buying things because they say to themselves, why should I buy today when I can buy tomorrow for cheaper? So the government will always institute policies that increase inflation. Which in turn will force the above trend in median earnings to continue to go down. Still don't believe me? Here's the proof:

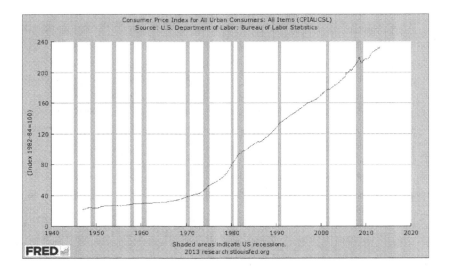

Inflation since 1940, courtesy of your local Federal Reserve bank:

Notice the small blip down in 2008/2009. We had a tiny bit of deflation. What was the result? The worst economic crisis since 1929, double-digit unemployment, and a declining middle class while the upper class got wealthier.

US household income

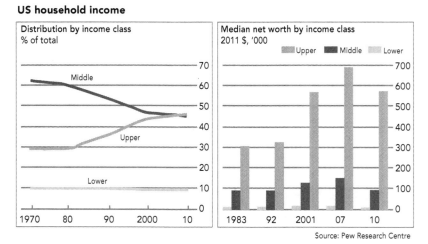

Source: Pew Research Centre

AN ASIDE:

Have you ever wondered why the stock market didn't just keep going down? Why it bounced at all from March 2009 until the day I am writing this, when the market is hitting all-time highs?

Very simple—and I state this with all humility—I personally saved the US stock market.

I moved to Wall Street in early March 2009. Specifically, the corner of Broad and Wall in the building that was once JP Morgan's bank. You may recall from your history books that the building was the site of the first major terrorist attack on the United States. On September 1, 1920, Italian anarchists exploded a bomb, killing thirty-eight, and injuring 143 (thank you Wikipedia. Thank you World Wide Web. Now I have every number I ever need for the rest of my life. My building, a bomb, 38 deaths).

About eighty-nine years later, at the worst possible time, someone decided to convert the building into apartments. The building had a bowling alley. A basketball court. A pool. A gym. And you couldn't give those apartments away. The building was a ghost town. NOBODY wanted to live on Wall Street. You couldn't find a more depressed group of people than the ones going to work every day at the New York Stock Exchange; why would any of them want to live next to it, too? It was the black hole of capitalism.

So, of course, I moved in. Directly outside my window: the world famous New York Stock Exchange. I looked to the right and there was Federal Hall where George Washington was sworn in as the first president of the United States. A huge flag lit up at night, projecting its negative shadow straight through my apartment. I loved it.

I loved everything about living there. I felt like part of history. Like maybe this would be a new start for me. Which was an odd feeling, because everything else was going to hell. The S&P 500 was heading towards a 20 year low, where it reached the magically hellacious number of 666. I was losing more money than I thought possible and going through a divorce. One time I made the mistake of looking at my bank account balance. I considered, once again, jumping out the window, or figuring out which drugs would anaesthetize me long enough that I'd never have to think about my problems again.

Then I lost my job. Nobody called me. Nobody wanted to talk to me because I was bullish on the market and everyone thought I was crazy. Certainly nobody wanted to help me make money. I was trying to get other companies started but people had their own concerns and I didn't have my health or priorities intact (as we will see later, those are critical for success). I was just as depressed as they were, and they were just as depressed as everyone else.

And it wasn't just that the stock market was at a low. That's too easy an excuse. The human race hasn't survived for 200,000 years just to be shattered by a little blip in capitalism.

We'd all had a tough decade. We all suffered from postsocietal traumatic stress disorder. The first step was admitting it: Internet bust. 9/11. Corporate corruption on a scale never before seen. Housing bust. Financial crisis. Bailouts. Madoff. On and on. It was rough. As a society we got afraid. Too afraid to move.

So I did the only thing I could do: I woke up early one morning in early March and bought a bag of chocolates. Small Hershey's chocolates, like you hand out on Halloween. At around 8 a.m., I stood outside the entrance of the New York Stock Exchange and started handing out chocolates to everyone walking inside. People would be staring at their feet like zombies as they walked in, but 100 percent of the time, they would stop, look up, take the chocolate, and they would smile.

Chocolate releases phenylephylamine, the same hormone that is released when you fall in love. Suddenly, for a brief moment, everyone in the stock exchange was a little closer to falling in love. This made them less likely to be depressed, at least that day. This is not to say you should eat chocolate all the time. You'll get obese. It's much better to just simply fall in love.

But we were having a hard month/year/decade right then and everyone needed a break. Everyone needed a piece of chocolate at the beginning of the workday.

It was March 9. A Monday. The Friday before, the S&P closed the week at its lowest point in thirteen years (and ever since). By the end of the week, the S&P was up nearly seventy-five points. By the end of the month, it was up more than 125 points. And it's been going up ever since.

I'm not trying to brag. I'm not trying to say how great it is that I saved the global economy. It's not bragging if it's true.

This is not a classist or communist argument. This is not about optimism or pessimism. More people are finding financial success than ever before while unemployment or "underemployment" (where people are employed, but at jobs paying less than they are accustomed to, that they are massively overqualified for) has reached upward of 20 percent

Does this mean the rest of us just die? Of course not. This isn't all doom and gloom. It's just reality. And it's actually good news. It's the decline of institutions that have lied to us for the past one hundred to two hundred years. It's a new reality that people who apply the principles in this book—who start carving their own path—can take advantage of.

Human beings are born pioneers. The rise of corporatism (as opposed to capitalism) forced people into cubicles instead of out into the world, exploring and inventing and manifesting.

The ethic of the Choose Yourself era is to not depend on those stifling trends that are defeating you. Instead, build your own platform, have faith and confidence in yourself instead of a jury-rigged system, and define success by your own terms.

It's time to get back to our roots. It's time to ride the surf as the ocean crashes onto the beach. Fight it, and the undertow of falling median earnings and a shrinking middle class will pull you down and drown you.

PERMANENTLY TEMPORARY

I recently visited an investor who manages more than a trillion dollars. You might think a trillion dollars sounds impossible. I did. But there's a lot more money out there than people let on. It's squirreled away by families who have been hoarding and investing and reinvesting for hundreds of years. And this trillion dollars I speak of belonged to just one family.

We were high up in the vertical City of New York. His entire office was surrounded by glass windows. He brought me over to one of them. "What do you see?" he said.

I don't know, I thought. Buildings.

"Empty floors!" he said. "Look at that one. Some bank. All empty." He pointed at another building. His fingers scraping across his window like...I don't know...whatever a spider uses to weave its web. "And that one: an ad agency or a law firm or an accounting firm. Look at all the empty desks. They used to be full, with full-time employees. Now they're empty and they will never fill up again."

I spoke with several CEOs around that time and asked them point-blank, "Did you fire people simply because this was a good excuse to get rid of the people who were no longer useful?"

Universally, the response was a nervous laugh and a "Yeah, I guess that's right!"

And because of the constant economic uncertainty, they told me, they are never going to hire those people again. Recently I joined the board of directors of a temporary staffing company with $700 million in revenue. The year before they had $400 million. That growth occurred in a flat economy. I now can see firsthand and immediately what parts of the economy are hiring full-time and what parts of the economy are moving toward using more temporary workers.

I'll tell you the answer: ZERO sectors in the economy are moving toward more full-time workers. Everything is either being cut back, moved toward outsourcing out of the country, or hiring temp workers. And this goes not just for low-paid industrial workers, but middle managers, computer programmers, accountants, lawyers, and even senior executives.

My investor friend was right.

The reality is that companies don't need to hire as much anymore because technology has reached its manifest destiny from the pulp science fiction novels of the 1930s. Essentially, robots have replaced humans. (The dream has come true! Cubicle slavery is finally over!) I saw this coming years ago. I used to work in the technology department at HBO right when the Internet was spreading across corporate America. It occurred to me then that nobody would need technology departments anymore. For one thing, at least one-third of the programmers were working on networking software. Well, the Internet is one big networking protocol. So all of those people can be fired. Another one-third of the programmers were working on user-interface software. Well, the web browser solves the entire user interface issue, so all those people can go, too.

This is just one example. But across every industry, technology has replaced not only paper ("the paperless office"), but people. Companies simply don't need the same amount of people anymore to be as productive as they've always been. We are moving toward a society without employees. It's not here yet. But it will be. And that's okay.

We're already seeing more startups than ever get funded, get customers, and pull business from the corporate monoliths, which have slept for too long. This isn't just about money, though. If it were, it would be boring. It's also not about being a great entrepreneur. I'm an entrepreneur, a writer, and an investor. Not everyone is an entrepreneur. Not everyone wants to be one.

This is about a new phase in history where art, science, business, and spirit will join together, both externally and internally, in the pursuit of true wealth. It's a phase where ideas are more important than people and everyone will have to choose themselves for happiness, just like I did. They will have to build the foundation internally for that choice to manifest. And from that internal health the rest will come, whether it's a business, art, health, success.

An example: Tucker Max is known for his "fratire" books. The titles of his first two bestselling books were *I Hope They Serve Beer in Hell* and *Assholes Finish First*. Both books sold millions of copies.

But he wasn't happy with that. The publishing industry was taking too big a piece of the pie. Their claim: that they handled distribution, editing, marketing, publicity and they paid advances. Tucker realized that because of modern technology, he no longer needed just about any of this. For a fraction of the cost, he could get editing, marketing, and publicity, and he simply bought the same distribution that the publishers would pay for. And because his prior books were successes, he didn't need the advance up front.

So he started his own publishing company, in effect, simply to publish his next book.

It was called *Hilarity Ensues*, and he took 80 percent of the revenues instead of just the 15 percent that publishers normally give. He chose himself and ended up making three times the money after all his costs.

This is now happening in every industry. The music industry has transformed. Artists go to YouTube to first get known and then they can skip the major labels altogether as their music gets sold directly on iTunes. We will see an example later on with the musician, Alex Day.

Authors like Tucker Max can bypass a five-hundred-year-old industry by using technology to make three times the money. Tech startups are forming at ten times the pace of the late 1990s. And they are actually generating profits and growing revenues at lightning-fast speeds.

You no longer have to wait for the gods of corporate America, or universities, or media, or investors, to come down from the clouds and choose you for success. In every single industry, the middleman is being taken out of the picture, causing more disruption in employment but also greater efficiencies and more opportunities for unique ideas to generate real wealth. You can develop those ideas, execute on them, and choose yourself for success.

The starting point for all of this is developing the inner perspective that allows you to choose yourself in the first place. Success by itself won't bring you happiness, because you can't do any of this from a position of ill health. If your body is sick, if you are around negative people who bring you down, if your idea muscle has not been refined into the perfect machine, and if spiritually you haven't developed a sense of gratitude and surrender, you will have less chances of success in the new Choose Yourself era.

"Wait a second," you might say. "Tucker Max wrote a book called *Assholes Finish First* about all the girls he was having sex with. How can you say he's worked on all of these areas of his life?"

One time I got upset when a well-known pundit tweeted that one of my books was crap. I asked her if she had read the book and she admitted, "No, I just didn't like the title." So I wrote a blog post about this.

Out of nowhere I got this e-mail from a fan of my blog who thought I was diving too much into negativity. And he was right. He wrote:

> "I assume your blog post was mostly tongue in cheek about the feedback affecting you in a negative way. But if not, then please take this compliment to heart: From one very successful writer to another, I love your blog. Yes, it has its quirks and stylistic issues, but it is utterly original and compelling, and that is an attribute that is incredibly rare. There is so much writing out there, and so little of it is worth a shit—but your blog is one of those that are worth a shit.
>
> I subscribe to like 25 blogs in my RSS feed, and yours is one. And I don't even really actively invest—I could care less about your financial advice.
>
> Please keep doing what you are doing, and please don't let the cowardly commentary from the ignorant sheep and trolls get you down. There are a ton of us out here that read

everything you put on your blog, and thoroughly enjoy it, but we don't tend to speak up one way or the other, because we're normal people with normal lives. Who even writes Amazon reviews? I've entertained millions of people, literally millions, but from my Amazon reviews you'd think my job was to punch babies in the mouth. That's the shitty part about the Internet, and about anonymous feedback, is that you tend to hear from the extremes, those that either love you more than reasonable, or those who are just spreading toxicity.

Fuck those people. You do great work, and I really appreciate it.

I hate to sound like a weirdo Buddhist, but the only things that really matter in this world are the relationships you have with the people you love, and the meaningful things that you do. Haters don't fit anywhere into that. Don't devote any mental space to them."

The e-mail was signed:
"Tucker Max"

In this new era, you have two choices: become a temp staffer (not a *horrible* choice) or become an artist-entrepreneur. Choose to commoditize your labor or choose yourself to be a creator, an innovator, an artist, an investor, a marketer, and an entrepreneur. I say "and" rather than "or" because now you have to be all of the above. Not just one. An artist must also be an entrepreneur. That's it. Those ARE your choices. Cubicles are getting commoditized. And when that happens, they empty out. I saw it with my own eyes when I visited my investor friend and stared out his office windows at the vacant vertical city.

And now I see it happening every day. It's not something that can be changed with laws or with printing money or with a change in values. It's history now. The world has already changed, and all the pieces are just falling into place.

Which side will you be on?

And Then They All Laughed

I liked this girl in summer camp when I was twelve. Of course when you like a girl there's an important protocol that has to be followed. You can't just tell the girl you like her. You have to tell your friend, who tells her friend, who then tells her, and then you get feedback. I put the plan in motion.

Sometime during "Art Group" or whatever it was called—I just remember I had paint all over my hands and clothes and face—the girl in question ran up to me and said, "I wouldn't go out with you in a hundred years!"

All the other kids started laughing. One counselor tried to calm everyone down and said, "Be nice," but of course nobody listened.

I watched the girl run out of the barn (where else would art group be?), paint all over me, the smell of a barn, the hearing of laughter—the only sense that isn't fully lasered into my memory right now is taste, and thank god for that because I'd probably just throw up.

I was rejected.

I remember thinking, One hundred years isn't so long, really. At least she likes me enough she'd consider me in a hundred years.

Rejection—and the fear of rejection—is the biggest impediment we face to choosing ourselves. We can all put together books about all the times we are rejected. We're rejected by lovers, by friends, by family, by the government, by the corporate world, by investors, partners, employees, publishers, and on and on.

> ▶ *Try this exercise:* Think for a second of ten different times you've been rejected. Were you rejected for a job? Did you have a novel rejected? Did a potential girlfriend/boyfriend reject you? List ten. Now think about this: how easy would it be to list one hundred? I can probably list one thousand.

But what if you never try? What if you are afraid to try for fear of being rejected?

I understand this. I've been rejected more than I care to remember; to the point where some days feel like enough is enough. When you put yourself out there on a daily basis, that's going to happen (whether you deserve it or not): you get hate mail, you get rejected for opportunities (even if accepted for others), you get people who don't understand you, who are upset with you, angry with you, don't respect what you've done for them.

You can't hate the people who reject you. You can't let them get the best of you. Nor can you bless the people who love you. Everyone is acting out of his or her own self-interest.

What you need to do is build the house you will live in. You build that house by laying a solid foundation: by building physical, emotional, mental, and spiritual health.

This is not some new-age, self-helpy jargon. "Be kind to people and all will be well." This is a book on how you can achieve success for *yourself,* and these are the building blocks. The phrase *financial freedom* includes the word *financial* but it also includes the word *freedom*: freedom to explore the blessings that surround us. Freedom to help ourselves so that we can help others. Freedom to live the life we choose to lead, instead of having to live the life that has been chosen for us.

This book will help you build the house where your freedom resides. Just know that the house does not exist in the past. It cannot be built where you are standing right now. It is *out there*.

Since the beginning of humanity, we've looked for frontiers. It is only a myth that we have evolved to a point as a civilization where we can count on safety. The only truly safe thing you can do is to try over and over again. To go for it, to get rejected, to repeat, to strive, to wish. Without rejection there is no frontier, there is no passion, and there is no magic.

How we deal with rejection is a combination of several factors. It's not just about how healthy we are mentally. Or how healthy we are psychologically and emotionally. There's the saying "Time heals all wounds." This is true. But we can control to some extent how much time it takes. It takes a different amount of time for each person, depending on the number of factors we allow to affect us.

We will see those factors repeatedly throughout this book when I describe in greater detail what I have referred to in previous books as the "Daily Practice," and when we analyze the stories of many others who have chosen themselves. Not because they wanted to, but often because they had to.

The key is building the foundation underneath. And then taking a positive action: to choose yourself.

Those with high levels of social anxiety about rejection are shown to have lower levels of a hormone called oxytocin. We are all born with different levels of this and other hormones that help modulate our reactions to different external stimuli relating to things from social anxiety to money to happiness to loss.

Oxytocin levels can be boosted by the foods we eat, how we exercise our mind, how we associate with others, and even is partly responsible for how we cultivate an attitude of gratitude toward both the positive and negative events in our lives.

The point is not that chemicals rule our lives. Quite the opposite. But in order to have a fully functioning life, we need a functioning body, a healthy brain, a functioning social life, a functioning idea muscle, and a very fundamental sense that there are some things we can't control. For instance, I couldn't force someone to give me a million dollars in 2002. Any more than I could force that girl to like me when I was twelve.

And obsessing on the things we can't control is useless. It takes us out of the game. We have to choose to be in the game.

Therapists might say, analyze the past to see where your current negativity comes from. Perhaps a parent rejected you as a young person and now you feel particularly sensitive around rejection.

This doesn't work. Dwelling on negativity won't suddenly have positive results. It only brings more negativity into your head. You can't buy happiness with the currency of unhappiness.

The idea that we need to "pay our dues" is a lie told to us by people who wanted our efforts and labor on the cheap.

You need to build a positive base: physically, emotionally, mentally, and spiritually. Once these four "bodies" are working in harmony, you can reach out into the world. You build the foundation for the house you want to live in.

Some people say, "Through rejection we find strength." This is most likely bullshit. Maybe you get some strength and you persevere. But it also hurts. I don't like to be rejected. There are self-help books like *Failing Forward* or *Excuses Begone* or other negative-oriented titles that embrace rejection and that basically say success is about 90 percent failure and 10 percent perseverance.

This isn't one of those books.

Here's what I believe.

We're taught at an early age that we're not good enough. That someone else has to choose us in order for us to be…what?

Blessed?

Rich?

Certified?

Legitimized?

Educated?

Partnership material?

I don't know. But this feeling of insecurity overwhelms us. When we are not chosen, we feel bad. When we are chosen— even by idiots—we feel like that one actress (I can't remember and I refuse to look it up) who said at an awards ceremony, "You like me! You really, really like me!"

Goldie Hawn? I forget.

We need to unlearn this imprisonment. Not dissect and analyze it. Just completely unlearn it.

When I get on a subway, I like to find a seat and read and daydream until I arrive at my destination. Who doesn't? Nobody likes to hang onto the crowded smelly poles, bumping into people, crowding together, shaking at each stop, trying to hang on for balance, for dear life.

What does this have to do with choosing yourself?

A very simple test was done by Yale psychologist Stanley Milgram. He took ten students and sent them on the New York City subway system.

They went on subways and walked up to all sorts of people who were sitting down: young, old, black, white, female, male, pregnant, etc. To each seated passenger they said, "Can I have your seat?" Seventy percent of the people gave up their seats.

Two interesting things: one, that the percentage of people who got up was so high. They were simply being asked to get up and they did as they were told.

But the other interesting thing is how reluctant the students were to even do the experiment. To ask people for their seats went against everything they had ever been taught. This is obviously an extreme. But it points out how hard it is for us to do things for ourselves unless we are given some implicit permission.

I'm not saying "Choosing Yourself" is equivalent to manipulation. I'm not saying it's equivalent to always getting what you want.

But understanding the rules of this Choose Yourself era that we now find ourselves in will give you the confidence and skill set to go out there and simply ask the world for your proper place in it. Without a doubt, you will get what you ask for. Not in a law of attraction sort of way, where the idea is you get what you visualize. That doesn't work without having all of the other pieces in place.

This book is about those other pieces, and getting them in place. It's about understanding the external myths that have broken down; the same ones that created the massive American middle class, which is now dying, and left us with the Choose Yourself era in the fallout. People are walking around blind. If you are the one who can see, you will be able to navigate through this new world. You will be the beacon that will enhance the lives of everyone around you and, in doing so, trigger the actual law of nature that says when you enhance everyone around you, you can't help but enhance yourself.

DOES ONE PERSON HAVE CONTROL OVER YOUR LIFE?

About twenty years ago, I realized I was tired of trying to be liked by others. I was constantly trying to package myself so I would be chosen for jobs, books, deals, partnerships, or love. Depending on the situation, I would put on an entirely new costume, a new mask, or a new set of lies, right down to political and religious beliefs. "Dan Quayle might be the greatest vice president ever," I said to one girl as she lit up my cigarette even though I didn't smoke, and I probably thought Dan Quayle was the worst choice for a vice president ever. And then when I leaned in for the kiss at the end of the date…"I don't feel about you that way." Rejected.

I suffered two other rejections that thoroughly disgusted me to the point where I said, "That's it. I'm choosing myself."

The first: I was pitching a TV show, *III:am*. Three a.m. The idea was to explore the flip side of life. From 7 a.m. to 8 p.m., the "normals" are outside, conducting their business. Dressing in their suits, getting the grande soy cappuccinos, kissing up to the boss, eating three meals, gossiping, watching TV, having a glass of wine at the end of a tough day, and finally cajoling themselves to sleep after tucking in all of their worries for another night of rest.

When "normal" human beings wake up at three in the morning it's usually because those worries have prematurely woken up before the dawn. "James! You have to worry about this." And when it happens, we tremble. There's absolutely nothing we can do at three in the morning about our regrets, our anxieties, our fears of loneliness or depression or poverty. The paranoia that creeps in from the cracks in the windows, from the cracks in our minds.

▶ Here's an exercise for those who typically wake up anxious and paranoid at three in the morning: instead of counting sheep to get back to sleep, count all the things you are grateful for. Even the negative parts of your life. Figure out why you should be grateful for them. Try to get up to one hundred.

But what about the people who live only at three in the morning? People who are out and about, conducting their lives every day at those hours. Living a life completely opposite of the "normal." I started going out at three in the morning on Tuesday and Wednesday nights. Not Saturdays, where everyone is out partying, but the nights where if you were around at three in the morning, there's a reason. And it's usually not a normal one.

What I found was more than just prostitutes, their clients, drug dealers, and homeless people (although I certainly found a lot of them—and throw in the pre-op transsexuals and dominatrixes for good measure). I also found a whole class of people who did not fit into the conventional path of life and had to carve out their own. A path that only existed when nobody else was looking, when the lights were out, when 95 percent of the world was asleep. It was almost as if a 3 a.m. religion existed, one that was self-reliant and relished how the world can be lived upside-down but still lived to its fullest potential.

For three years I interviewed people every week for the HBO website. During one of those years, I also took material and shot it as a pilot for HBO. HBO was very excited about it and threw some money behind the pilot.

Then they rejected it.

There was ONE executive at HBO, in particular, who could make or break my project with a simple "yes" or "no." I was constantly afraid of her and what she was thinking. What would her mood be every time we went in with a new update?

Finally she gave her verdict: "For material like this, you either need to show your neighbors fucking, or someone killing their mother while naked." We had material pretty close to that but not quite as base or lowest common denominator.

We were rejected. All it took was one person on a bad day. She was, and I think still is, head of HBO's Documentaries and also head of HBO Family Programming. The shows your kids watch.

The second: I was trying to sell my first company. We had one potential buyer. I never even considered trying to get other buyers. They were going to offer $300,000. I had about $500 in my bank account. I had never sold a company before. I knew nothing about business at all, in fact, and yet we had built up a solid, little business that was doing well.

Every day I would dream about it. I thought with a little bit of money in the bank I could take a year off and write a novel. Or two. Or do a TV show. Or quit. Or whatever.

They seemed as enthusiastic about the deal as I was, so I assumed that the money was in the bank without ever looking for other opportunities. Big mistake. When you give up searching for frontiers, inevitably you end up stuck in a swamp, sinking deeper into the mud the more you struggle to get out. I'm not sure that analogy holds, but you get what I mean. Success comes from continually expanding your frontiers in every direction—creatively, financially, spiritually, and physically. Always ask yourself, what can I improve? Who else can I talk to? Where else can I look?

Lo and behold, after months of due diligence and negotiation, the company that I wanted to buy us, rejected us. I felt horrible.

Both of these situations happened at basically the same time, and for the same reason. In each situation my entire happiness seemed dependent on the decisions of one person. I gave power to that one person to make or break my life.

Of course, both rejections worked out better for me; they always will, for reasons that have to do not only with perseverance, but quantum physics, health, spirituality, being a real human, and many other things that I will discuss in this book.

But the most important thing these rejections gave me was a sense that NEVER AGAIN should I rely on the whims of one person to choose my success or failure in any endeavor.

And did that attitude work?

Of course not. It's like telling someone with hundreds of thousands' worth of plastic surgery to instantly go back to looking how they used to look. Their body no longer knows how.

I kept kissing ass. I kept falling down. I kept being dishonest to my needs inside.

It took me a long time to begin the practice that really indoctrinated me into the Choose Yourself era. This book is about those practices so you can hopefully skip the years it took me to choose myself.

The ability to choose yourself—an ability that is now being forced on us for historical reasons discussed in the last chapter—is the result of a comprehensive framework of health that must be practiced to be experienced, and must be lived to be fulfilled. If you don't like what I recommend, don't do it. But it worked for me and all the times I've been down on the floor. It's been the only way I've been able to get back up.

No matter how hard it tries, a ripple that laps onto the shore will never be as powerful as the ocean that created it. The goal is to be the ocean—the central force in our existence that moves mountains, creates all life, shakes continents, and is respected by everyone.

This book is about becoming the ocean. About choosing yourself to be the ocean. So everything that you do emanates out like ripples, everything you do moves the earth, and enhances your life and the lives of all the people around you.

Now, let's enter the Choose Yourself era.

How to Choose Yourself

～

I'm an addict. For twenty years I replaced one addiction with another. I can't even describe all of them. I'm actually embarrassed. Ashamed.

I would cling to whatever addiction was making me happy at that moment. A fire sucks the oxygen out of everything in the room. When the oxygen is gone, the fire is extinguished. Then burnout occurs. That's addiction. It takes every form: entrepreneurship, drugs, sex, love, games, and escapism of all forms. I've been addicted to all of them. I've even been addicted to the 12-step meetings where you get to meet the other people who might be as screwed up as you are.

Addictions: let's work a hundred hours a week for fame, money, sex, health, more fame, then F-you money, then stand on our heads, then get fancy artwork, big houses, guard dogs, pit bulls that kill people, bigger bank accounts. Heck, let's own the bank. Then let's double down on all of the above.

Now there is a new addiction. "All I want is freedom," a lot of people say. But freedom from what? Who is enslaving you that you can't get away from? Then people want freedom for their kids, or their parents, or their siblings, or their kids' kids. Or five generations of kids. Where did all these kids come from?

But still, "It's all for them. Everything I do."

Then we get burned out. Too much fighting for freedom. Who were we fighting all of that time? When all that time we were free without realizing it. There are no chains on me as I write this. But the feeling is immense: all I want is freedom.

There are two very important basics for harnessing that freedom and succeeding in the Choose Yourself era. There's no avoiding them. There are no excuses for not doing them. The good news is they are free.

ONLY DO THINGS YOU ENJOY. This might seem obvious to you, but it isn't to most. One might also say, "Duh, I'd love to do what I enjoy but I have to pay the bills!" Relax for a second. We're going to learn how to do what we enjoy, first. I'm not just talking about those "only pursue a career you enjoy" platitudes, either. I mean it down to your very thoughts. Only think about the people you enjoy. Only read the books you enjoy, that make you happy to be human. Only go to the events that actually make you laugh or fall in love. Only deal with the people who love you back, who are winners and want you to win too.

This is a daily practice.

I only just started doing this in the past few years after being infinitely unhappy, getting divorced, losing money, losing jobs, careers, friends, everything I was clinging to. Eating a turkey sandwich in a diner by myself on Thanksgiving Day 2008, I said, "Fuck it." I was done.

I used to go out every night. You never know, I would think. I used to go to every business meeting I was invited to. You never know, I would think. I used to go on TV every time I was asked. You never know, I would think. Maybe someone would SEE me. And call me and offer me and give me and want me and like me and love me. Maybe they would press the LIKE button on my face. Brilliant.

[Note to self: invent TV sets with "LIKE" buttons so people can LIKE people they see on TV and that somehow gets transmitted back to the TV networks.]

Ninety-nine percent of meetings don't turn into money. Ninety-nine percent of the news is a lie (trust me. I know them). Ninety-nine percent of TV is about scandal, murder, and cheating. Ninety-nine percent of the people on the street will lick the flavor right off your Life Saver if you let them.

Every time you say yes to something you don't want to do, this will happen: you will resent people, you will do a bad job, you will have less energy for the things you were doing a good job on, you will make less money, and yet another small percentage of your life will be used up, burned up, a smoke signal to the future saying, "I did it again."

The only real fire to cultivate is the fire inside of you. Nothing external will cultivate it. The greater your internal fire is, the more people will want it. They will smoke every drug lit by your fire. They will try to ignite their own fires. They will try to light up their own dark caves. The universe will bend to you.

Every time you say yes to something you don't want, your fire starts to go away.

You will get burned out.

You can say, "But what if I have to say yes to something I don't want to do?" Fair enough. We have mouths to feed, responsibilities, retirement to save for, and many things that might keep us in the prison of "No." Don't worry about that yet. The Daily Practice plows the field, and makes everything clear so that you'll know if your "yes" or "no" comes from a place of deep, internal satisfaction.

THE DAILY PRACTICE. You are empty. I mean this literally. Our bodies are like little galaxies. Galaxies have billions of massive stars in them and yet the reality is that the space between those stars is so gigantic that a galaxy is mostly empty.

That's exactly like you. You are made up of atoms. Every piece of you. *And yet the actual physical matter in an atom (protons, neutrons, electrons) take up only one-fiftieth of one percent of the space in that atom.* The rest is empty.

So you are empty. There's nothing really there. The real you—the real fire—is inside this emptiness.

We spend our lives afraid of the emptiness. We want to fill it with love, with money, with pleasures, with anything that could put off the ultimate. But all of those things are never enough. They all decay.

Only the emptiness does not decay.

The best way I have ever found to fill that hole is not to seek external motivations to fill the emptiness, but *to ignite the internal fire that will never go out.* To light up my own inner sky.

So how do you do this?

Picture your body for a second. You have a heart that pumps blood one hundred thousand times per day, or seventy-two times per minute, sending 1.3 gallons of blood through your body. If there's any blockage—in a vein or an artery—you'll die very quickly. Within minutes. That's a heart attack. Blood cleans the system, sending water, oxygen, and nutrients to every part of your body.

All you need to do to live longer is to constantly make sure you are doing everything you can to protect your heart and the blood that flows through it. This is a function of diet, exercise, sleep, and other things. If the heart gets sick, you die. When you finally die, make no mistake, it will be because the heart got sick.

Imagine now you have three other bodies alongside your physical body:

- an emotional body
- a mental body
- and a spiritual body.

Imagine a life force that flows between them and through them, much like blood. Imagine a central core that must keep everything healthy. Just like you must keep your heart healthy to live a long, productive, and even happy life, you must keep these other bodies healthy as well and exercise them on a regular basis. A daily basis. A minute by minute basis.

I call this the Daily Practice.

This might sound corny. It might sound like mumbo-jumbo. I don't know. I don't care. It's a method of thinking that works for me. Other techniques might work for other people. Good luck to them. This works for me.

In the next chapter, I'll describe a simple Daily Practice to start off with. But below is the best way to keep these bodies healthy. It is from a foundation of health (in all four bodies) that you build the platform to choose yourself. The rest of the book describes how one can use this foundation to build the succeeding layers to create even more choices that lead to success. And you'll read stories of people who have done just that.

THE PHYSICAL BODY. The shell that we must take care of to live. It houses everything we do. And it's pretty simple. We know when we are doing bad things to it. Too often we think, "Once I achieve X, Y, Z, goal, I'm going to get back in shape." But it doesn't work that way. Not that you need to be ripped and jacked or eight-packed or whatever. You just need to be healthy. And you know what I mean?

You need to shit regularly. That's it.

And how do you do that?

You don't eat junk food. You sleep seven to nine hours a night. Avoid excess alcohol. Exercise. And by exercise I don't mean run eight miles a day. I mean take walks. Can you take a ten-minute walk every ninety minutes? Can you take a twenty-minute walk? Can you use the stairs instead of the elevator? Do five minutes of yoga?

My routine: Wake up somewhere between 5 and 6 a.m. Mostly protein breakfast (I like Tim Ferriss's slow-carb diet that he describes in his book *The 4-Hour Body*), and a late lunch around 2 or 3. Lots of walks and breaks while I walk. You can never get enough exercise really, and no creative person has ever complained about too much walking. And then I go to sleep between 8 and 9. Nobody ever died of starvation avoiding that third meal of the day. And if you eat too late in the day, or drink alcohol too late in the day (which pretty much wipes out drinking alcohol at all), your body gets into trouble digesting at night. Which will hurt your sleeping. Which will hurt your metabolism in the morning. And so on.

THE EMOTIONAL BODY. Emotionally I try to surround myself with only positive people who inspire me. This way I can learn to be positive. To be a beacon to those around me.

It's important to avoid people who bring you down. Not in a cruel way. But avoid engaging or overly dwelling on people who are constantly draining you of energy. A friend of mine is starting up a company as I write this. One of his partners is constantly criticizing him. Every time I talk to him he says, "ABC is at it again. Here's what he said now." And he goes into a long diatribe of the latest crimes against humanity his partner has committed.

The key is: acknowledge that the person is driving you crazy. You can't suppress that. But with observation, the pain will begin to wither. And the less you engage with the person, the less overall effect that person will have on you. Even if that person is close to you (and they often are. That's why they get to push all of those buttons), find out ways to not engage. Say hello in the hallway, smile nicely, but no engagement. Put a quota on yourself how much you can complain or feel anxious about that person in a day.

You can't be beautiful unless you get rid of the ugliness inside. People become crappy people not because of who they are, but because they are crapping inside of you. Stop letting that happen.

> ▶ Here's an exercise I do that can help in this regard: I try to be quiet. Instead of speaking the average 2,500 words a day that most people speak, it would be nice for me to speak just one thousand words a day when possible. This forces me to carefully choose my words and who I engage with.

THE MENTAL BODY. Your mind desperately wants to be the BOSS. It needs you to be very, VERY BUSY with BS stuff so it can do all the things it's good at: obsess, worry, fear, be depressed, feel exuberance, forward thinking, backward thinking, thinking thinking THINKING until...

burnout.

So you need to tame the wild horse or it will tame you until you are a slave. Nobody wants that. The way you tame it is through focused use. Set a goal: I'm going to come up with ten ways I can have more time for myself. Or I'm going to come up with ten ways I can make my job better. Or ten business ideas. Make sure the list you plan to do is a hard one. You need to make the mind SWEAT so that it gets tired. So tired that it's done for the day. It can't control you today. TIRE IT OUT! Then do it again. Ten MORE ideas. I discuss this much more in the section "How to Become an Idea Machine."

I'll tell you what I did today. An online education company asked me to come up with an online course. Maybe I'll do a course on "The Daily Practice," but I made a list of ten other courses I could maybe teach. It was hard! I didn't even know if I knew enough about ten different topics to be able to teach them. I still don't know. But I made the list. My mind sweated like a pig. And then you know what I instantly did afterward?

I fell asleep.

After sleeping about ten hours the night before. Sleeping is fun. I love to sleep. It's a Saturday. It was 1 p.m. I took a half-hour nap. My mind was tired. Then I woke up and wrote this. Come up with ten ideas a day.

THE SPIRITUAL BODY. Most people obsess on regrets in their past or anxieties in their future. I call this "time traveling." The past and future don't exist. They are memories and speculation, neither of which you have any control over. You don't need to time travel anymore. You can live right now.

When I walk around New York City, everyone seems to have glazed eyes. They are walking around in the past or the future. They are time traveling. One exercise I try: look at the roofs of buildings. Finding the art in the city around me is a good technique to keep me right here, when everyone else is in the time machine.

I have money worries. I have relationship fears. I have insecurity. Will they like me, hate me, love me? Will I ever go broke? Will Claudia ever leave me, like so many others have? All fears from the past, all worries of the future. I have regrets. Maybe if I had been a better parent...maybe if I had been a better son...maybe if I hadn't lost all that money I could've saved lives...maybe, maybe, maybe.

All of that doesn't exist. It's my mind pretending they exist.

I give up. I can't control the past or the future. They are empty, just like I am. All there is is now.

Done.

When you surrender and accept the beautiful stillness around you, when you give up all thoughts of the past, all worries and anxieties of the future, when you surround yourself with similarly positive people, when you tame the mind, when you keep healthy, there is zero chance of burnout.

How do you surrender? By trusting that you've done the right preparation. You've done all you can do. All that is within your power, your control. Now, give up the results. The right thing will happen.

This is the ONLY way I've ever ignited the fire and avoided burnout. Think about the things we worry about. How, almost 100 percent of the time when we look back on a particular fear, we realize how useless worrying about it was.

This doesn't mean you will never be in a bad mood. Of course you will! That's what the body and mind does for a living: it goes back and forth between good moods and bad moods. The trick is to recognize a bad mood, say, "I'm in a bad mood," and wait it out. So you can get back to enjoying things. So you can get back to making decisions and making choices, but only when you are in a good mood—a mood where you are fully present and not time traveling.

Devoting yourself to a Daily Practice helps to build incremental improvements in our lives, even if you only notice the tiniest increments at a time. Today they will build up. Every moment they will build up. Every moment they will shed the extra garbage that you carry with you on every level, the garbage that weighs you down, the external garbage that eventually catches on fire, burning you OUT, on the outside.

Instead, igniting the fire on the inside burns a light so fierce it can't be burned out. Instead, you will brighten the galaxy. You will add brilliance to the lives around you. You will become a beacon, a light that attracts abundance, instead of a flickering fame that is eventually smothered.

THE SIMPLE DAILY PRACTICE
(or Why Do So Many People Want to Die)

A lot of people want to die. And I don't blame them. The most dreadful thing in life is not dying. It's being born. Once you are born, you're screwed. Now you have to actually survive. You have to grow from someone who craps their pants, can't speak to anyone without crying, and can't walk or feed themselves, to a full-grown adult who can barely do all of that while also juggling a mortgage, a marriage, kids, career, whatever, to finally being an old man who can't do any of those baby-like things again.

Then you die. No worries after that.

How do I know a lot of people want to die? Because Google tells me. The search phrase that is most likely to take people to my blog is, "I want to die." The number-two search phrase is "I hope to die." Number three is "How can I disappear," which is a little more hopeful than dying but expresses no less similar a sentiment (it's sort of like saying "How can I kill this life I have and start another"). My e-mail is slightly more uplifting. The most popular question I get via e-mail is "I'm stuck. How can I move forward in life?"

Each of those last people is not quite at the "I want to die" point, but somehow their lives have stalled. The reason they're stalled is because the axis of the world has changed. We can't rely on the job, the marriage, the relationship, the house with the white-picket fence, the college degree, the anything external for that matter. Nothing counts. Everything we dreamed for was an illusion.

So people find themselves on the floor. Without "a life," as they put it. They obviously have a life. They are breathing. But they don't know how to choose life for themselves. The masses rely on others to do it for them. They have given up their Life to live a smaller "life," ruled by others.

I get that. It's happened to me over and over again.

But this reliance on others has to come to an end. It was always a myth. Everything we hoped for. The society that we were told would be here, waiting for us, is completely gone and is never coming back. You can either take the blue pill (become depressed about an artificial reality that is never going to return) or take the red pill (fully enter the Choose Yourself era and take advantage of its opportunities).

And it's not as if our bosses will help us. They hate us. No matter how nice they are to you, they actually hate you. The head of a major news organization asked me to breakfast a few months ago. He wanted advice on how to build up the traffic for his company's website. When I say a major news organization, I mean MAJOR. You read his newspaper every day.

We started off with his version of idle chitchat. "I'm having a problem with my reporters. They all get Twitter accounts and then the ones with a lot of followers suddenly want raises and promotions."

"Why is that a problem?" I said. "Don't you want your reporters to be widely liked and respected?"

He gave the typical BS response. "We're about the news. Nobody is a star."

That's the problem. A corporation wants identity to go away. He wanted his best and his brightest to be mediocre so that the corporation, not the individuals inside of it, would burn bright. What's going to happen is that his company will lose, and all of his "stars" will go supernova on their own.

Why do I put so much emphasis on the Daily Practice? Am I trying to sell a religion or something?

No, I put emphasis on it because it's the only thing that's ever worked for me. Following that practice is the only thing that "unstuck" me, pulled me off the floor, saved my life, and actually propelled me to success.

And since I've been writing about it, I've seen it with thousands of others who have written me e-mails about it. I've collected testimonials, some of which you'll find at the back of the book. Those weren't tweets or e-mails I got over a period of a year. Those were tweets and e-mails I got over a period of the past hour as I wrote this.

I'm not selling anything (well, this book in your hands, but if you know someone who can't afford it, then please let me know and I will send it to them for free). In fact, I encourage people to not believe me. All of the people who are stuck or frustrated or scared or anxious or filled with regret, please try these ideas so you can see for yourself.

This is how we form a better society. First we become better as individuals. You can't help others if you look in the mirror and hate what you see. And it's very easy to hate what is there. We live most of our lives hating the mirror. Heck, I'm pretty gruesome to look at in the morning. It's a daily challenge!

Many people say, "The Daily Practice is too much work for me. I can't do it all every day."

No problem. Let's first define the "Simple Daily Practice," then we can go into more of the subtleties.

Why the need for a simple daily practice?

I went to a talk given by my friend Ramit Sethi who wrote the bestselling book *I Will Teach You to Be Rich*. Ramit and I have gone to each other's talks several times and we've also done a few videos together. He takes a behavioral psychology approach to personal finance that I think is very unique. It's not the simple "save an extra $1,000 a month and you will be rich." In fact, he took a survey of personal finance authors who recommend that people keep budgets, and he found that none of them actually kept budgets themselves.

In his talk he made a point that was near and dear to me. Claudia, my wife, had been trying to get me to floss my teeth. I get lazy and I try it for a few days but then get tired of trying to dig into all the little areas in between my teeth. It's like a half-hour process, so after a while I stop and then after a few days I give up. When Ramit started talking about flossing, I saw Claudia's ears practically twitch.

He said the way you get people to floss is to just ask them to floss one tooth. That's it.

Suddenly, they are "flossing." Their brains say, "I'm the type of person who likes to floss." Maybe after a day or two they start flossing two teeth. "And why stop there?" Ramit said. "After a few weeks, they're flossing all of their teeth because their brain sees it wasn't as hard a habit as they thought."

The Simple Daily Practice is the same. All you really need to do to get off the floor is acknowledge that it's not your external life that needs to change (you have little control over that), but that external changes flow from the inside.

External changes in your life are like the final ripples of the ocean that lap onto distant shores. A promotion, a raise, a new job offer, a new relationship. These are the final ripples. The ocean is inside you. Becoming aware of that infinite presence doesn't require meditation in a cave for fifty years. It involves simply being healthy. Healthy not just physically but emotionally, mentally, and spiritually.

For now, the Simple Daily Practice means doing ONE thing every day.

Try any one of these things each day:

A) Sleep eight hours.

B) Eat two meals instead of three.

C) No TV.

D) No junk food.

E) No complaining for one whole day.

F) No gossip.

G) Return an e-mail from five years ago.

H) Express thanks to a friend.

I) Watch a funny movie or a stand-up comic.

J) Write down a list of ideas. The ideas can be about anything.

K) Read a spiritual text. Any one that is inspirational to you. The Bible, The Tao te Ching, anything you want.

L) Say to yourself when you wake up, "I'm going to save a life today." Keep an eye out for that life you can save.

M) Take up a hobby. Don't say you don't have time. Learn the piano. Take chess lessons. Do stand-up comedy. Write a novel. Do something that takes you out of your current rhythm.

N) Write down your entire schedule. The schedule you do every day. Cross out one item and don't do that anymore.

O) Surprise someone.

P) Think of ten people you are grateful for.

Q) Forgive someone. You don't have to tell them. Just write it down on a piece of paper and burn the paper. It turns out this has the same effect in terms of releasing oxytocin in the brain as actually forgiving them in person.

R) Take the stairs instead of the elevator.

S) I'm going to steal this next one from the 1970s pop psychology book *Don't Say Yes When You Want to Say No:* when you find yourself thinking of that special someone who is causing you grief, think very quietly, "No." If you think of him and (or?) her again, think loudly, "No!" Again? Whisper, "No!" Again, say it. Louder. Yell it. Louder. And so on.

T) Tell someone every day that you love them.

U) Don't have sex with someone you don't love.

V) Shower. Scrub. Clean the toxins off your body.

W) Read a chapter in a biography about someone who is an inspiration to you.

X) Make plans to spend time with a friend.

Y) If you think, "Everything would be better off if I were dead," then think, "That's really cool. Now I can do anything I want and I can postpone this thought for a while, maybe even a few months." Because what does it matter now? The planet might not even be around in a few months. Who knows what could happen with all these solar flares. You know the ones I'm talking about.

Z) Deep breathing. When the vagus nerve is inflamed, your breathing becomes shallower. Your breath becomes quick. It's fight-or-flight time! You are panicking. Stop it! Breathe deep. Let me tell you something: most people think "yoga" is all those exercises where people are standing upside down and doing weird things. In the *Yoga Sutras,* written in 300 B.C., there are 196 lines divided into four chapters. In all those lines, ONLY THREE OF THEM refer to physical exercise. It basically reads, "Be able to sit up straight." That's it. That's the only reference in the *Yoga Sutras* to physical exercise. Claudia always tells me that yogis measure their lives in breaths, not years. Deep breathing is what keeps those breaths going.

Anyway, this isn't advice for the one-hundred-thousand-plus people this past year who typed "I want to die" into Google and ended up on my blog. Some of them probably need real help from a therapist or doctor.

But this is what I did when I wanted to die. **Every one of these things.** At least one item a day. And here I am. I am still alive.

What if I'm in a Crisis?

Before we hit the stories in the rest of this book, we have to handle the situation when we're actually on the floor and it seems like there is no way up. We can't do the full daily practice, no less our "one thing per day," if we can't even get off the floor.

Sometimes flossing one tooth to start isn't enough. Sometimes you're in agony, your teeth are about to fall out, and you don't want dentures. Flossing will have to wait.

I've been in that situation. And I'm not talking metaphorically, I'm talking about my actual teeth being in such bad shape they were about to fall out. But I'm also talking about when life hits a little too hard, a little too fast (okay, now I'm talking metaphorically).

Sometimes it's enough to just climb out of bed. To be grateful for the abundance already in our lives. And abundance is a tricky thing. Right now, look around, and list the areas where you are abundant. If you are in the middle of a rainstorm, there is an abundance of water. Think of the bounty that can be grown with that water. If you are in a traffic jam, there is an abundance

61

of cars. Think of the human achievement those cars represent in our short history on this planet. Turn despair on its head.

With each obstacle, turn it into a moment where you can reflect on the bounty that is in your life.

I recently got the following e-mail:

"So…I'm slowly starving to death, I have –$90 in the bank account, rent is due in 8 days, and I have no chance of paying it. I started two media businesses that failed miserably and no one wants to hire me. What should I do?"

My response:

"That sucks. And I mean it. I've been there. And not so long ago. It fucking sucks. Sorry for the language. You didn't use bad language in your e-mail so I apologize.

If I tell you what worked for me, would you try to do it? Even if it won't work (you're not going to pay your rent in 8 days. That ship has probably sailed but who knows.).

It's all going to sound corny. Because you are in a fight-or-flight mental state. And if something says, "Slow down," your body and mind will want to reject it.

A) Can you call some people today and tell them you are grateful for them. Because this is the abundance in your life. You're old enough that no matter what has happened in the past, there are people you are grateful for. Please call them. Family, friends, ex-clients, ex-lovers. Whoever. And tell them why you are grateful for them. What you learned from them. Why you love them.

B) You are very lucky. You have time on your hands. Can you try to spend one afternoon volunteering? You're probably spending a god-awful amount of time thinking about yourself. Just one afternoon, volunteer someplace else. Please. This is abundance also. You have two hands and two legs and a brain. People with less need your help.

C) See a doctor. I know you aren't sick. But you probably aren't sleeping. You need to sleep. Ten hours a day. Maybe nine. But no less than nine. There are so many benefits to sleep. Google it and see. It's amazing how I don't have to list the benefits anymore. They are somewhere on that THING, Google. Doctors help you sleep. There are various pills that work. Don't get addicted to them. Just use them until the crisis is over. Anyway, I'm not a doctor. The doctor will tell you that. Ask for Klonopin and see what they say. Don't forget: YOU ARE NOT DEPRESSED. It's perfectly reasonable to be upset in your situation. But you are anxious. So an anti-anxiety pill will help you sleep.

D) You have to exercise. Even just take a walk. Twenty minutes of exercise a day. How come? I have no clue. But it works. Ugh, it brings to mind when I was worried about rent checks and divorce checks and girlfriend checks and my checks and I had nothing and I would exercise and it would feel like shit. But you have to do it. Your body is getting constantly mugged right now, triggering that fight or flight. So you have to work it off somehow. Exercise, eat well, and sleep. Else your body will be upset and then you will feel worse.

I just gave you a lot of things to do. Which is hard. Because who needs more shit on their plate. So you have to replace some things with these things. No news. No TV. No junk food. No dinner if you can avoid it (eat a late lunch and a late breakfast. And why not—you're not at a job).

I would say get rid of the worries, but that's really hard. I can say, whenever you worry, replace it with thoughts of abundance. Sometimes this works. But it's really hard to do and most people find it corny.

Please do the things on my list, though. They are all equally important. You might not see it now but if you do this list, things will be better. Please write me back in eight days and tell me what happened. But make sure you do the things on my list."

Eight days later he wrote back, "Thanks! Guess what? I paid the rent. I'm still alive."

That's it. I didn't ask for details. Sometimes emergency procedures are required. But then you have to get back to living. You have to get back to the basics of how to survive. Let's see some examples.

CHOOSE YOURSELF TO LIVE

Kamal Ravikant went missing. We had been corresponding for more than a year, ever since I started my blog. I'm very grateful for the great friends I have met through my blog. It has been a totally unexpected but much appreciated benefit of writing.

After hundreds of e-mails back and forth during the prior year, I was finally visiting San Francisco and was getting all set to meet Kamal. But he didn't show up for our planned breakfast. His brother, Naval, called him a few times. "He's at home," Naval said, "but he's not picking up. His illness must be overwhelming him today." Naval had a GPS specifically attached to where Kamal was.

Kamal was very sick and getting worse. This had been going on for months. Some days he couldn't move or wake up. Other days he had enough energy to go outside but only for minutes and then he had to go back inside. Kamal's sickness was chronic. The doctors couldn't help him; he was infinitely tired, feverish, in pain, and it was getting worse.

I knew from our correspondence that Kamal had been going through a hard time before he got sick. His company, which had once been doing well enough to raise a significant amount of money, was faltering, perhaps failing. He had recently broken off a relationship. A close friend had died.

Often when we attach our happiness to external goals: financial success, relationship success, etc., we get disappointed. Even when things work out, everything cycles, and the happiness is often fleeting.

When those goals break, the external pain immediately gets reflected into our internal bodies. Our emotions break. We feel sad, disappointed, and in pain. We cling to the past happiness, or our hoped-for goals, which now have to change. It can feel like your arm is being torn off your body.

But Kamal was trying to hold it all together to be fair to everyone within his company—the employees, the investors, and the customers. He was clinging to the past, depending on the future. Clinging to everything and everyone except for his own happiness in the present.

His emotional body couldn't handle it anymore. His emotional arms and legs were torn off. And then his physical body broke. He completely broke down. I noticed he had dropped out of touch a few months earlier and I hadn't seen his comments on the blog in a while. "What's going on?" I wrote him. "I'm sick," was his reply. He dropped out.

For several months he was out of action. Then he started writing again and telling me what was going on in his life. He started commenting on the blog again and interacting with the great community developing there. He was alive again. We finally ended up meeting.

"How'd you get better?" I asked. "What happened?"

"I'll tell you the secret," he said, "I thought I was going to die. I was just lying in bed and couldn't move, I had a high fever, and was in too much pain. I really thought I was going to die. Finally, *I just started saying over and over again, 'I love myself.'*"

As Kamal then wrote about his experience in the now-successful book, *Love Yourself Like Your Life Depends on It*:

> *And I got better. My body started healing faster. My state of mind grew lighter. But the thing I never expected or imagined, life got better. But not just better, things happened that were fantastically out of my reach. This I couldn't have dreamed of [...] I found myself using the word 'magic' to describe what was happening. And through it all I kept repeating to myself, 'I love myself. I love myself. I love myself.'*

In the book Kamal describes his transition from sickness into health and the other magical things that happened to him. He also gives a series of techniques and practices so you can try this for yourself. And finally he answers the dreaded question, what happens if you don't love yourself? Can you still get this magic into your life?

"Think about it," he said to me months later when we met in New York. "When someone is in love, they almost magically look better. I needed to be in love with myself to feel better. So much of what had happened had weighed on me until I collapsed. Now I needed to love myself. It became a mantra for me."

As someone explained to me the other day, the word *mantra* has two parts (in Sanskrit): "man"—thoughtfulness with zeal, and "tra"—to protect. So by saying "I love myself" over and over, Kamal was protecting the thought, nourishing it, and the love was nourishing the rest of his body, his emotions, his mind, and his spirit.

Kamal is now completely recovered. He also figured out the situation with his business, and when I saw him in New York City it was as if a gigantic weight had been lifted off his shoulders.

How did he publish his book? He didn't need a publisher to choose him. He didn't need an editor to say, "It has to be 200 pages." He didn't need a marketing expert to put it in a few bookstores, where it would waste away. The same way he chose himself to LIVE (by forming his own personal Daily Practice) he chose himself to write and, to this day, continues a pattern of choosing himself for success. His book went on to become a bestseller. And he did it all himself. Just like Tucker Max did. Just like I do, and did with this book. Here's how you can do it:

How Do I Self-Publish?

There are lots of variations on the path to self-publishing; this is the one Kamal and I have both used.

WRITE THE BOOK. Kamal wrote his in a few weeks and made it forty pages (nobody had to give him permission to make it a smaller book). For my last two, I took some blog posts, rewrote parts of them, added original material, new chapters, and created an overall arc related to what the books were about to give them a trajectory, or a direction. It doesn't matter where you get your ideas or how you write them, just do it. That said, you probably already have the basic material.

CREATESPACE. Both Kamal and I used CreateSpace because they are owned by Amazon—where we were going to sell our books—and have excellent customer service. They let you pick the size of your book, and then have Microsoft Word templates that you download to format your book within. Kamal did his all himself. I did my first book by myself, as well. But for my second book, for a small fee, I hired someone (Alexanderbecker. net) to format the book, create the book design, and create the final PDF, which I uploaded. He also checked grammar, made proactive suggestions on font (sans serif instead of serif), and was overall just extremely helpful.

UPLOAD THE PDF. CreateSpace approves it, picks an ISBN number, sends you a proof, and then you get to approve the proof.

WITHIN DAYS, IT'S AVAILABLE on Amazon. And you're a published author. It's print-on-demand as a paperback. And by the way, your total costs at this point: $0. (Plus whatever you used to design your cover.)

KINDLE. All of the above (from CreateSpace) was free. Kamal had a friend design his cover as a favor. If I didn't hire Alex to make the cover, I could've used one of the million possible CreateSpace covers (I did that for my first book) and the entire publishing in paperback would be free. But with Kindle, CreateSpace charges $70 and they take care of everything until it's uploaded to the Kindle store. Now your book is available in paperback *and* Kindle editions.

MARKETING AND PROMOTIONS. You're in charge of your own marketing and promotions (as opposed to a book publisher). This might sound daunting at first, but self-publishing is the essence of creative entrepreneurship, and entrepreneurs can't use the excuse that "I don't have time, I'm running a business." This is your business. Entrepreneurs make time. Like the publishing process itself, marketing and promotions can take many forms as well, depending on your goals, so this is just what Kamal and I did.

Kamal reached out to his entire network. He had various friends (including me) blog about it. Bestselling author Tim Ferris tweeted how Kamal's book brought him out of a funk. Before you know it, Kamal's book was a bestseller and, as of this writing almost a year later, it's still selling strong.

I did a bunch of different things.

1. I gave away the first twenty copies or so to readers of my blog who asked for one. Many of them then posted good reviews on Amazon to get the ball rolling.

2. I handed out the books at speaking engagements.

3. I wrote a blog post about how the book is different from the blog and why I chose to go the self-publishing route.

4. I wrote guests posts for blogs like Techcrunch, which helped immensely and for which I'm very grateful.

5. I used my social networks: Twitter, Facebook, Linkedin, Google+, Quora, and Pinterest.

If you have a story to tell or a service to offer (it doesn't matter what), love yourself enough to choose yourself. Take control of your work, your life, your art. The tools are out there. Now you just need to use the tools inside yourself.

I'll let a quote from Kamal's excellent book close this chapter:

> *If a painful memory arises, don't fight it or try to push it away—you're in quicksand. Struggle reinforces pain. Instead, go to love. Love for yourself. Feel it. If you have to*

fake it, fine. It'll become real eventually. Feel the love for yourself as the memory ebbs and flows. That will take the power away.

And even more importantly, it will shift the wiring of the memory. Do it again and again. Love. Re-wire. Love. Re-wire. It's your mind. You can do whatever you want. [...] The results are worth it. I wish that for you.

FINDING YOUR PURPOSE IN LIFE

When I was twelve years old I had one purpose in life—other than getting the girl in art group at summer camp to like me. I wanted to be a colonel. And not just any colonel; I wanted to be an honorary colonel in the Kentucky State Militia. Just like my hero, Colonel Sanders. I had to start off slow—Kentucky was the glamour state to be a colonel of. First I started off with Mississippi. I called the governor, Cliff Finch, and interviewed him, because for some reason that I still can't figure out, he was running in the primaries for president against another former Southern governor and incumbent president, Jimmy Carter.

Cliff Finch invited me down to Mississippi. His campaign and my dad split my air fare, about $60 each. It was the first time I had ever been in a plane and I was scared. When I landed everything looked the same but people talked differently. It was a weird feeling. As if I had landed in an alternative universe. The main things I remember from that trip were getting the certificate that made me an honorary colonel of the state (I better get an eighteen-gun salute the next time I fly there!), presenting to Governor Finch how he would win the "youth vote," and a lot of people asking me what it was like to be Jewish.

Then I wrote to the governor of Alabama and I told him my family was moving to Alabama, I had read everything about Alabama and I loved the state and now I wanted to be a colonel there. The governor sent back a huge certificate: James Altucher was now a lieutenant colonel in the Alabama State Militia. In Texas, I became an honorary citizen. In North Carolina, I became an "honorary tarheel." But with Kentucky, I couldn't crack the code. They knew how valuable their colonelship was. They needed references, background checks, etc. I was twelve years old and decided for the first of many times to quit while I was ahead. Still, if anyone wants to call me "Colonel" (Mississippi), I'm totally fine with that.

Which brings me to an important point. Probably the most important person in Kentucky history is Harlan Sanders, the man himself, the colonel, the "inventor" of Kentucky Fried Chicken, one of the most successful franchise operations in history. Extra-crispy Kentucky fried chicken still has to be one of the best foods on the planet. You might get sick afterward, but who cares. Buddha says live in the now!

A lot of people say to me, "I'm twenty-five years old and still have no idea what my purpose in life should be." When Colonel Sanders was twenty-five, he still had yet to be a fireman, a streetcar conductor, a farmer, a steamboat operator, and finally proprietor of a service station, where he sold chicken. The chicken was great and people loved it but he didn't start making real money until he started franchising at the age of sixty-five. That's the age he was when he found his "purpose" in life.

I don't like the word *purpose*. It implies that somewhere in the future I will find something that will make me happy, and that until then, I will be unhappy. People fool themselves into thinking that the currency of unhappiness will buy them happiness. That we have to "pay our dues," go on some sort of ride, and then get dropped off at a big location called our "purpose," where now we can be happy.

It doesn't work that way.

You can find the tools to be happy right now. I still don't know what my purpose is. I'm afraid I will never know. That makes me very happy. Maybe I can have lots of adventures between today and the day I die. Maybe I can do lots of different things. And if I don't—if I die even tomorrow—that's fine also. What does purpose mean when we are dead? We might as well choose to be happy now.

Other people have found success after changing careers many times: Rodney Dangerfield didn't succeed in comedy until his forties. One of the funniest guys ever, he was an aluminum siding salesman. And then he had to start his own comedy club, Dangerfield's, in order to actually perform as a comedian. He chose himself to succeed! But not until his forties.

Ray Kroc was a milkshake salesman into his fifties. Then he stumbled onto a clean restaurant that served a good hamburger run by two brothers with the last name McDonald. He bought McDonald's when he was fifty-two.

Henry Miller wrote his first big novel, *Tropic of Cancer*, at age forty.

Raymond Chandler, the most successful noir novelist of all time, wrote his first novel at age fifty-two. But he was young compared to Frank McCourt, who won the Pulitzer for his first novel, *Angela's Ashes*, written when he was sixty-six. And, of course, Julia Child was a young fifty when she wrote her first cookbook.

One of my favorite writers of all time, Stan Lee, created the entire universe for which he is known—the Marvel Universe—when he was forty-four, inventing Spiderman, the Fantastic Four, the Avengers, and others along the way.

If you don't like to kill people but still need a weapon to immobilize them, consider the Taser, invented by Jack Cover when he was fifty. He didn't sell a single one until he was sixty.

If you like restaurant reviews you might have read *Zagat*, started by Tim Zagat, who quit his job as a lawyer in order to create the book of reviews when he was fifty-one.

Harry Bernstein was a total failure when he wrote his best-selling memoir, *The Invisible Wall*. His prior forty (forty!) novels had been rejected by publishers. When his memoir came out, he was ninety-three years old. A quote from him: "If I had not lived until I was 90, I would not have been able to write this book, God knows what other potentials lurk in other people, if we could only keep them alive well into their 90s."

Peter Roget was a mediocre doctor who was finally forced to retire in his early seventies. Then he became obsessed with words that have similar meanings. Was his "purpose" as a medical practitioner or as a guy who could play with words? Do you know him as a doctor or as the author of *Roget's Thesaurus*, which he wrote when he was seventy-three?

When I was in college, I ate ramen noodles every day for year. One time in a grocery store a woman tried to tell me they were the worst thing I could eat. Really? Like worse than eating a brick, for instance? That was when I was nineteen. I'm now forty-five. It doesn't seem to have hurt me that much to have eaten ramen noodles for an entire year. It was the only thing I could afford. If something costs 25 cents and has a few slivers of peas in it, then it's okay by me. Meanwhile, the inventor of ramen noodles didn't invent them until he was forty-eight years old. Thank god for him!

Charles Darwin was a little bit "off" by most standards. He liked to just collect plants and butterflies on remote islands in the Pacific. Then he wrote *Origin of Species* when he was fifty.

To top it all off, there's Henry Ford. He was a failure with his first car, the Model T, which he invented when he was forty-five. He didn't yet have the productivity efficiencies of the assembly line. He developed those when he was sixty.

This is not meant to be inspirational. You might never have that "great" thing you do. I'm not even saying it's the journey that one should love, because some journeys are very painful. And nobody says you get special marks in death if you wrote a great novel at the age of fifty. Or came up with a great chicken, or a way to stuff lots of people into factories. I've stumbled and fallen and gotten up and survived enough that I'm sick of goals and purposes and journeys. I want to cut out the middleman. The journey. The desperation and despair that focusing on "purpose" entails.

Forget purpose. It's okay to be happy without one. The quest for a single purpose has ruined many lives.

Someone asked on Quora, the Q&A website, recently, "I feel like a failure for being 27 and not knowing what I want to do in my life. What should I do?"

My response was that when I was twenty-seven, I had yet to start a business, yet to ever fall in love, yet to write a book, yet to make a TV pilot, yet to fail at twenty businesses in a row, yet to run a hedge fund, VC fund, even become a chess master (which happened at age twenty-eight for me). Most important, I had yet to fail. But I failed so much in my thirties that I practically forgot I was a chess master. As I write this, I'm forty-five and I still have no idea what I want to be when I "grow up." But I'm starting to finally accept the fact that all I want to be is ME.

Meanwhile, Harlan Sanders made such a great chicken that, even though he'd barely made a dime off of it (that happened fifteen years later), at the tender age of forty-five, the governor of Kentucky made Sanders an honorary colonel.

So I guess at age forty-five, there's still hope for me.

How to Disappear
Completely and Never
Be Found

We get stuck. We get unhappy. Maybe we're in a hopeless marriage. Maybe a hopeless job. Maybe you picked up this book and you are thinking to yourself, "Well, this is all good but it's too late for me."

I'm sorry if you feel that way. I've felt that way many times. Sometimes you wish you could start fresh, with no responsibilities, an empty canvas you can now paint or repaint your life against. I've been feeling this way, on and off, for at least twenty years. As I mentioned before, the third most popular search phrase that takes people to jamesaltucher.com is "I am stuck." When we feel stuck, we want a massive change, we want the entire world to reverse its rotation and drop us off at an entirely new place. I tried that more than once.

In 1992 I wanted to move into a homeless shelter because I thought that girls who were homeless would be more likely to go out with me. I had this fantasy version of what a homeless shelter would be like. We'd sneak around to each other's rooms as if they were dorm rooms. It would be romantic. Lots of giggling. And crack smoking. Heck, I'd try it. For love.

I had a job and wasn't really homeless. I had a place to live. But my girlfriend at the time hated me and I needed a change. Plus the homeless shelter was right next to my place of work. I could've lived at the shelter and it would have been about a twenty-second walk to work. How great can life be? I ask again: how great can life really be?

The homeless shelter director said no to my request. I told him I wanted to write about the experience. He called my references. My boss—my ACTUAL boss at the time—said I was probably mentally ill. I didn't have that job for too much longer. Nor did I move into the homeless shelter. They actually thought I was too deranged to move into a homeless shelter.

All of this is to say, there's something primal in me that wants to disappear. To mix with what I view as the lowest of the low, to forget about my past, to sign up for a future that is meaningless, to think only about right now and give up everything else.

People build up a life, it becomes unsatisfactory, and they want to figure out how to change it like an outfit on a doll.

But you can't change life from the outside. We all know this now. In the Choose Yourself era, it is only possible to give up the normal contraptions of externalized identity and live a life more free than you can imagine if you start from the inside out. Maybe you can't live "off the grid" (unless you like a place like Montana. Good luck with that) but you can live a life of unexpected surprise. Where every day is an adventure. And every time you look in the mirror, a new person is there.

When I was a kid, I bought the book *How to Disappear Completely and Never Be Found*. I don't know if any of the techniques still work but here was the author's plan:

Look at old newspapers from around the day you were born to find the names of babies that died that day. Ask members of your state government for their birth certificates. This isn't unusual. Many people lose their birth certificates. Use the birth certificate to get a Social Security card (say you've been a permanent student up until now). Use the two forms of ID to get a bank account, credit cards, and driver's license.

Change your hair color. Lose weight. Put a tack in your shoe so you start to walk differently. Start siphoning money out of your bank account until it is all in cash. Find a crowded city where you can rent an apartment cheap, and disappear in the crowd. Plan on building an employment history by starting with temp or construction jobs.

Then disappear. Just walk out of your house and never go back. You've just committed pseudocide.

The word *pseudocide* fascinates me. It's like a "little death," a phrase often used to describe an orgasm.

The book had anecdotal stories of people who had disappeared (how the author kept finding these people was never explained). People running from marriages, lawsuits, the IRS, or maybe just every now and then someone who needed an eraser, some Wite-Out to rub over emotions, fears, and anxieties. A clean slate that would bring a temporary nirvana where some, if not all, of the mental and emotional baggage can be discarded with your old life. Wrapped up in a garbage bag and left behind a bowling alley.

The feeling never left me. When I'm in an unfamiliar neighborhood, I look around and judge whether or not I could disappear there. Would people find me? Would I ever run across someone I knew or who recognized me? Could I just be swallowed up by the chaos here, live in a shelter, work temp jobs in the back of a deli, and argue in broken Chinese in some broken-down Chinatown?

Think of the mass appeal that a TV show like *Mad Men* has. It's not for the allure of 1960s advertising culture. It's for the fresh start the main character, Don Draper, has given himself. Don Draper, of course, lives a secret identity. And one of the best episodes to ever appear in television history was the episode "The Jet Set," where he lived a secret identity within a secret identity—when he just simply disappeared while standing in the lobby of a hotel in California and went off with a bunch of wealthy vagabonds, each with infinitely long back stories that we would never know and never hear of again. By the time Draper emerged from this new identity, he found himself wealthy, divorced, and dealing with the questions we all grapple with: who are we, really?

I have baggage. I have people I care for. Other people I'd rather avoid. I have things I hope for. I have goals and ambitions. I have grudges. No matter how much of a minimalist style you want to have, you are still stuck with all these things in your head, for better or for worse.

What if you could just wake up in a new place and all the baggage was gone? What if you decided, "You know what, these goals aren't worth it. Too many people die while climbing the perilous mountain of their goals." When you are young, you think you can climb that mountain. But when you start to get a little older you realize, "Damn, if I fall now that's a long way down."

Disappearing into the depths of some ghetto, satisfying only your minimal needs, using your aura of mystery to acquire minimal friendship, and just living each day as it is dealt to you, may solve most of these issues. But they probably won't. The question is: with your current identity, can you live as if you've already disappeared? We all want to de-clutter. To throw things out. But a minimalist lifestyle is bullshit unless you can do it across every sheath in the daily practice: not just physical, but also emotional, mental, and spiritual.

More important is to throw away the baggage, the grudges from the past that, a thousand years from now, will mean nothing. Give up on the ambitions for the future that are more trouble and anxiety than they are worth. To de-clutter your brain. To be free. To suffer a "little death" or to be "born again."

Meditation Exercise: Picture yourself in a brand-new identity. Truly homeless. A vagabond. A nomad. Imagine you have enough in the bank. Imagine your prior responsibilities are all taken care of. You can go to India and live there for twenty years on almost nothing. Nobody knows who you are. You are brand-new. It's as if you woke up in a new body. You have no connection to the past and no goals for the future. Really picture every detail of it. When I visualize it, I feel a great weight lift off my shoulders. I want to feel that way all day long. Tell me the truth: how do you feel?

But Really, Can I Disappear?

Assuming you have the basics down, the freedom described above, is it possible to get the freedom that disappearing implies?

The answer is yes. In fact in the Choose Yourself era, you will have no choice.

You might not be able to live "off the grid"—we are beyond issues of privacy—because your every move is constantly tracked. But who cares? Do you think the government really cares about you?

The key is to *make money* off the grid, to make money outside the imprisonment of corporate America and out of the reach of the powers that choose or reject us. To be able to work from any location. As we move toward the employee-less society, where ideas become currency and innovation gets rewarded more than manual or managerial services, you will have the opportunity to live a life you want to.

In *I Was Blind but Now I See*, I wrote about how people no longer needed a home or an education. How both are leashes that society has created to hold you down and prevent you from growth.

But let's take it one step further. Do you need to even rent? Do you need to stay in one place? Maybe if you have kids and the kids are going to a public school (though I'd recommend *unschooling*, but that's an entire other book[1]) then you might be tied to one place.

Otherwise, the entire dream of technology's full potential has finally come true. It hasn't just created efficiencies at the workplace. It's created efficiencies at home, as well. Earlier I stated that the rise in technology was partly the cause of the era we now find ourselves in—being forced out of the nest so we either fly or die.

But ultimately it's our ever-increasing quest for a frontier—physical, technological, material, and spiritual—that creates the opportunities for those who hunt for them.

---

[1] Start with my book *40 Alternatives to College*, which could just as easily apply to high school.

We still live in a consumption world, where people continue to accumulate computers, cars, TVs, furniture, etc. But none of it is necessary.

You can move from place to place using services like AirBnb, which find very nice, furnished places for you almost any place in the world for relatively cheap prices. You can use services like Zipcar to find the closest car, with key in the ignition for you, to take on your extended trips.

When I travel using AirBnb and Zipcar, I bring almost no luggage with me. I don't need a computer or a tablet because phone sizes now are almost as big as mini-tablets. And anytime I need a computer, there's usually a convenient FedEx Kinkos around from which I can use to write articles. All of the books I would want to read are on my "phablet" (my phone/tablet, which is the Galaxy Note II). Almost any work-related tools I need are stored within apps on my phone. The only thing I can't do with the phone is write, but that's where FedEx Kinkos comes in.

And what else do I need? What else do I need, ever?

Well, you might ask, what if you have a job?

Get rid of it. You ultimately don't need it. You ultimately will be pushed out of it. We've already talked about it. We're already living it. Cubicles have become commodities. Whoever sits in a cubicle becomes replaceable. I've seen it with my own eyes.

You might say, "But I can't get another job just like that. I can't quit my job."

Fine. Don't. Do the Daily Practice instead. It will be like magic, I promise you. You will find another job. You will find the right places where you belong. You will find ways to develop alternative sources of income so your reliance on one source of income diminishes. The opportunities are there, you just need to be flexible and fluid enough to take advantage of them.

I'll give you one example. A friend of mine created a database of all houses in the United States that are "rent to own." In other words, they are for sale, but the owner is willing to rent the houses until the rent paid in equals the price he would've gotten for the house.

How did he create the dataset? He basically looked at about a dozen other databases keeping track of all housing data and scraped specifically the rent-to-own houses off of them.

A lot of people in this economy are looking for rent-to-own houses. Banks aren't lending money and since incomes have fallen versus inflation (as we move toward the employee-less society) people don't have the money to make down payments.

So he solved a problem affecting a lot of people. He advertised on Google by buying keywords like *rent to own*. In order for someone to look at his database, they have to buy an annual subscription. Since people could potentially spend hundreds of thousands on the right house, they were willing to spend a few hundred on a subscription to his database, which he updates every day with new listings.

Last month when I called him, he had made $300,000 from his database. I tried to call him the month before that, but I couldn't reach him. He was on vacation in Greece. For the entire month.

I'm not suggesting people utilize this idea. By the time you read this book this idea might no longer exist. But there are other ideas. Other things you can sell. Before the rent-to-own idea, my friend was selling subscriptions to an online discount club, which searched the web every day for interesting discounts.

One person was disgusted when I told him about all of this. He said to me, "If everyone thought that way, then the few people who remained property owners would completely exploit everyone else."

The good news is that there are 250 million people in this country. Maybe more. I forget. And only a few of those people will read this book. Even if the book is a bestseller. And only a few of those people will follow this specific advice. It's not easy. Particularly if you have families, jobs, etc.

These are just seeds to be planted. Most people will not follow this particular advice. But I hope everyone follows the advice of the Daily Practice, where you internally get healthy enough to make the decisions about what is right for your life instead of relying on century-old customs and antiquated ideas about "property rights," "education," "jobs," "politics," and so on that have kept people enslaved with ancient philosophical shackles.

The planet is at a tipping point. Spiritually we need to recognize the importance of wanting less in our lives, to the point that we want to disappear. Technologically, we have the tools to make a living anywhere we want. And most of those tools fit inside a device that fits inside our pockets. Being physically, emotionally, and mentally healthy will allow you to combine the spiritual with the technological and sculpt the life that most satisfies you instead of the life that most satisfies society. Don't think, "I can't come up with an idea." You're getting ahead of yourself. Get all of the bodies aligned first. Later in this book we will learn how to develop the Idea Machine so you can start coming up with these ideas. But trust that when the foundation is built, the rest will follow.

And ultimately, a happy you will be the greatest contribution you can make toward a happy society.

Just Do It

I called up a plumber. Let's call him Mike X. Like Malcolm X but with a "Mike." "Is it really that great to be a plumber?" He was silent for a second and then a sort of gruff voice, "Excuse me?" he said.

"Sorry," I said, "I didn't mean to just blurt out a question. I'm writing an article. People keep saying, plumbers make a ton of money and make their own hours, etc. Is it really that great? I want to find out."

"Heheh. You tell that to a plumber who gets a call at 3 in the morning from some lawyer because the toilet in his guest room doesn't work and now has to get up and clean someone's pipes because they can't take a shit without their shower filling up with shit water."

"What do you mean? How does that happen?"

"Only so much can fit through pipes. And some things are not meant to go in pipes. People think they can do it themselves but there's only so much Drano you can use if seventy condoms are clogging the pipes."

"Jesus, are people having that much sex?"

"Heheh, I'm only speaking from experience.

"So I have to go down there and get out the stuff that never should've been there in the first place but has built up over years. And then when it forms a wall in the pipes, you also have to clear out everything that's backed out behind it. If it backs up enough then it's going to end up breaking the pipes and getting in other parts of the house, where it never should be. Or it drips onto your downstairs neighbor's living room carpet or whatever.

"So I gotta crawl in there and clean out condoms, lots of condoms, blood, hair, tampons, and then shit. Lots of shit. I've had my hand on so much shit it's as if I've wiped a thousand different asses other than my own."

"But is the money worth it? Are you your own man?"

Mike paused.

"I guess you can say that. I get to take off sometimes in the middle of the day. I went to watch my kid's Little League practice the other day."

"Are you happy?"

"It's not as bad as I am making it sound. Every situation is a different problem, and I like solving problems. It makes me feel like a detective. And I'm very good at it. But let me tell you something. Nobody wakes up in the morning and says, 'I can't wait to clean out some shit today.' I've never heard any of my buddies who are plumbers say that. But what you learn is that you do the job and you try to make sure you are happy in other parts of your life so the job doesn't get you down."

Inner balance. Inner health.

I'm sick of people saying entrepreneurs have it tough. And, by the way, that includes me. I've written it plenty of times. I'm sick of me doing it. Here's what I never wanted to do in my life:

- be a plumber
- work in a cubicle (although I did for many years)
- be a temp staffer (although I was)

I LIKE TO:

MAKE MY OWN HOURS. There's the myth that entrepreneurs work twenty-four hours a day. This is horseshit. Most people, entrepreneurs or not, waste time. After starting up several businesses, I can tell you this: I have never made one dime by traveling. And yet, I've traveled to most continents for business, cross country many times, meetings all over the place. No money from any of them.

One time I put up a map on our wall and pinned all the places my first company had "offices" and clients. I was walking a prospective acquirer through the room and pointed out the map. He stood there for a while, looking at it. He was sixty-five years old and had been running his own business for almost forty years. He said, "I find that there's usually enough business right here to make me rich." We were standing in the center of New York City, the richest city in the world! Why the hell did I ever have to go to Paris, where it's almost impossible to set up a business, to find clients? He called bullshit on me and he was right. And then he bought my company. Thank god!

Now I've learned the "Power of No." If someone asks me to go someplace, have a meeting, have a coffee, get on a call, etc., my first instinct is to say no. Much more value is created when I do the things I enjoy, when I work on my own creativity and continue to build the foundation for health. Rushing around the world trying to capture every piece of business will only result in financial and spiritual poverty. It's much better to work smarter, not harder.

HELP PEOPLE. Here are the people who it's in your control to help when you are an entrepreneur:

a. Your employees. I always have the philosophy that I want my employees to call home at the end of a hard day's work and say, "Mommy, I have the best job on the planet. My boss is great and I can see myself ten years from now running my own business. I'm learning so much." And you know what? Most of my ex-employees are running their own businesses now, too.

b. Your clients. You want them to look good in front of their bosses. How do you do it? Simple:

i. Do what they say.

ii. Do it on time.

iii. Do a little extra to surprise them.

iv. Give them ideas for how their jobs can even be better. Never forget sales rule #1: Your best future clients are your current clients.

v. Make their lives better. Listen to them. Go to their charity events. Introduce them to potential spouses. Introduce them to new jobs because you will have a bird's-eye view of the entire job landscape in their industry. These are not just your clients of the month: these are your clients for life. You are on this planet to serve them and make their lives better. I've had clients stick with me from one business to the next, even in totally disparate areas. You're never going to lose touch with the lives you save.

DEAL WITH CLIENTS I LIKE. It's horrible to deal with clients you hate. That's like the plumber waking up at 3 a.m. to clean the shit from a condom-flushing lawyer's pipes. I've had to do that. I've had clients call me up at three in the morning asking me for job advice. I've had clients call me up literally asking me "Do you like me?" I've had (I'm counting them in my head now) at least seven clients call me up asking me for bribes if I wanted more business. Did I pay? Of course I paid! I had employees to feed.

For a while I had a three-strikes-and-you're-out policy. If a client wasted my time on three deals where I didn't make money, then he was out. But I broke that rule too many times. Now I basically have a one-strike-and-you're-out policy. When I look at the ways I've been ripped off by potential customers (doing work on "spec," doing a deal where red flags were flying but I was overwhelmed by the dark side of the Force or whatever it was that made me part with my money, etc.), I'm really embarrassed. To think I paid for a great steak dinner for six just so I could hear a pitch about a time machine and a device that makes black holes. I'm about to sue myself right now.

BE ARTISTIC. Being an entrepreneur means you're going to create something in a way that a customer can't get anywhere else. Creation is art. It's how ideas collide in your head, then how materials collide to make your ideas real. Then it's how people collide to bring your creation to life in the real world with real users. Then it's how so much value is created so people are willing to spend money on it. How can you create that value? If you can ignore the petty worries. If you look out your window first thing in the morning and find beauty in the silence. The silence is the only place your creative ideas will come from.

MAKE A LOT OF MONEY. A lot of money. Let's be real. That's the main reason to be an entrepreneur. "But the economy?" someone might say. There is more money floating around than ever before. And a lot of that money is buried and hidden from you. Time to reach out and touch it. The stock market has a capitalization of several trillion dollars. There's another $2 trillion in private equity funds. There's $50 trillion in transactions in the global economy every year. If you make money, someone will buy your company. Or, even better, you'll make so much money so fast you don't have time to sell your company.

Yeah, it's hard. It's stressful. Your employees will have sex with each other and then cry. People will talk about you behind your back. You'll miss payroll. Your customers will drop you. Your investors will hate you every now and then. The key is to always have the base foundation built; your physical, emotional, mental, and spiritual bodies need to be healthy and flowing with each other. This will provide the foundation from which your ideas will get generated, solutions and opportunities will appear almost magically in the face of the problems that inevitably arise for all entrepreneurs, and everyone around you will feel the benefits.

DEAL ONLY WITH COLLEAGUES I LIKE. There's that test: only hire someone you wouldn't mind sitting next to on a plane ride across the country.

Better, then, to be the one hiring than the one trying to be hired. When you are trying to get hired, you put on the mask that says, "I'm the guy who you will like to sit next to flying across country." I don't like putting on masks. Nor do I like the people around me to put on masks. It's very hard to see through all the costumes. People don't even know they are wearing them; they go through so much of their lives pretending to be someone else, someone who is liked, instead of being who they really are.

COME UP WITH IDEAS. When you work at one job, you come up with ideas for that one job. That's fine. Nothing wrong with that. I'm not criticizing working for a big company (although I will. Stay tuned.). But when you have your own company, it never stops.

If you have a product company, you come up with additional features to put on your product. Every day. Then you spec it out. Assign it to someone to do it. Put a time line on it, and check in every day until it's done. Then you roll it out. See how people use it, tweak it. Build a fan base around it. It feels really good to see someone using what you made.

If you have a service company, you come up with more services. For instance, if you are helping companies post to Facebook, how about you also help companies build an e-mail list out of their millions of Facebook fans?

No matter what, every day you are coming up with ideas to transform your business. When I was running Stockpickr .com, I wanted to create a fund that would invest in the top ideas from the top investors. When I was running a web services company, we almost went into the rap label business, the movie business, the tea business (!), the data business in about ten different areas. In retrospect, some of our ideas were great and we had the software to do them. I wish I had the business sense back then to really pursue some of the ideas. But I didn't.

If an idea didn't bring in money every month, then it was out. I never raised a dime for that business.

For my next business, I raised $30 million out of the gate, and eventually pulled together $100 million. What happened? Well, it was a bad idea.

NOT BE AT THE WHIM OF ONE DECISION MAKER (i.e., if you have a boss. Or if you have only one big client, who then basically becomes your boss).

I hate to beg. I hate to look at someone and think to myself, "If only they say 'yes' my entire life will be better." I hate to be nice to someone just so they like me and say yes to me and whatever I'm offering. I bet there are some prostitutes out there who like their job. I don't know. But I'm not one of them. I hate having sex with people I don't love. And that's what happens when one decision maker has control over your financial future at any moment in time.

BE AROUND LIKE-MINDED PEOPLE. In every business, I've loved meeting my competitors. The reality is there's no such thing as competition. The world is big enough for two people in the same space. If it's not, then you are in the wrong business. Your sector should be big enough for a hundred competitors. That's great news. It means you're probably going to make money.

In every business I've been involved in, I've gone out of my way to meet my competitors over breakfasts. I always learn so much: how they build up (their "secret origin" story that every superhero and every entrepreneur has), how they get past certain hurdles, how they handle difficult clients, what clients they can throw me (!), do they want to get bought, how much do they think they are worth, how do they get customers, and on and on. Even now I'm not in any one business, but I like to meet successful bloggers, authors, and angel investors. I learn from all of them and build good friends. This is how you build your "tribe." Your tribe, in part, is defined by you (you seek them out) but also defines you (you're in the tribe of entrepreneurs or you are in the tribe of cubicle people).

BE AN EXPERT. When you start a business and you have a service or product that is good enough for people to use over other similar products or services, then you are now an expert in your space. Even if you are new to the space, you're an expert. I like that feeling. I like giving talks. I like writing about the areas that fascinate me. I like starting businesses or being involved in sectors of industry that fascinate me. Sometimes you shouldn't be an expert and yet you still are.

When I started 140love.com, a dating service for people on Twitter, my site failed miserably. I was actually invited to give a talk at a Twitter-related conference. The title of the talk was "Twitter and Love." I was going through a divorce, and I had been dumped by four or five girlfriends in a row. Now I was supposed to give a talk about love. The irony is so thick I could spread it on sandwich bread if bread wasn't so high in carbs.

Anyway, that business died fast. And I didn't show up for the talk on the day of the conference. They had to find a quick replacement. Sorry, Jeff Pulver. He never invited me to speak at a conference again.

ONE LAST THING. I've discussed the reasons why this major paradigm shift is occurring. It's not that the system is out to get you. Or the system is imploding. This is not a conspiracy theory about the government or capitalism or the "1 percent." This is actually a great opportunity for people who can now navigate the rough surf that history is throwing up on our shores.

Regardless, you need to change for the changes that are coming. Some of these reasons I've covered in the preceding chapters, but I will go over all of them again so you don't have an excuse for not remembering them.

1) **The middle class is dead.** I laid out all the statistics and anecdotes earlier. Again, I don't say this as something to be scared of. And maybe I'm saying it a little too harshly. But at the current rate of incomes, and with the flight of capital out of the United States, you have to take this into account when making major life decisions. It's not like you can choose for this to not happen. It's not a choice. This is happening. In fact, it's already happened and we are all the Walking Dead.

2) **You've been replaced.** Technology, outsourcing, a growing temp staffing industry, and productivity efficiencies have all replaced the middle class. The working class. Most jobs that existed twenty years ago aren't needed now. Maybe they never were needed. The entire first decade of this century was spent with CEOs in their Park Avenue clubs crying through their cigars, "How are we going to fire all this dead weight?" The year 2008 finally gave them the chance. "It was the economy!" they said. The country has been out of a recession since 2009. Four years now. But the jobs have not come back. Everyone is getting fired. Everyone is toilet paper now.

   Flush.

3) **Corporations don't like you.** This is not a surprise to capitalists and entrepreneurs or even artists. The entire idea behind a corporation is to set up a legal structure that

takes advantage of cheap labor. The cheap labor makes something for you for less than you sell it. I'm not saying this isn't unfair. It is what it is. But you have to make sure if you are being exploited that you learn how to exploit back. You use the corporate job as a rest stop on the way toward being healthy, on the way toward figuring out how to innovate and take advantage of the mythical safety net to move onto bigger and better things.

4) **Money is not happiness.** A common question during my Twitter Q&A, asked at least once a week, is "Should I take the job I like or should I take the job that pays more money?"

Leaving aside the question, *should I take a job at all?*, let's talk about money for a second. First, the science: studies show that an increase in salary only offers marginal to zero increase in "happiness" above a certain level. Why is that? Because of this basic fact: people spend what they make. If your salary increases $5,000, you spend an extra $2,000 on features for your car, you have an affair, you buy a new computer, a better couch, a bigger TV, and then you ask, where did all the money go? Even though you needed none of the above, now you need one more thing: another increase in your salary, so back to the corporate casino for one more try at the salary roulette wheel. I have never once seen anyone save the increase in his salary.

In other words, don't stay at the job for safe salary increases over time. That will never get you where you want—freedom from financial worry. Only free time, imagination, creativity, and an ability to disappear will help you deliver value that nobody ever delivered before in the history of mankind.

By the way, this is not just an opinion. We can look at one simple profession: the law.

Lawyers are ranked number one in average pay. They are also ranked as the number-one profession for the percentage of people in that profession who are clinically depressed.

Of course, money can solve a lot of your temporal problems, and your worries in the material world. But it tends to magnify the big internal ones as well, the bad qualities.

5) **Count right now how many people can make a major decision that can ruin your life.** I discuss this in the chapter "And Then They All Laughed." I bring it up again so you can't escape it: how many people do you have to kiss ass to in order to achieve career goals? One? Two? The point here is to not kiss ass at all. To know that there are at least twenty people who independently can help you to achieve the success you need.

You build up this list of twenty people the old-fashioned way—you help them. The only way to create value for yourself is to create value for others.

▶ *Exercise:* think of two people in your network who don't know each other but you think can add value to each other's lives. Introduce them. Do this every day.

Get better and better at it. The more value you bring to the people in your network (even if it doesn't directly bring value to you in an immediate way), the greater the value of your network. And then the greater value you will have.

6) **Is your job satisfying your needs?** I will define "needs" the way I always do, via the four legs of the Daily Practice. Are your physical needs, your emotional needs, your mental needs, and your spiritual needs being satisfied?

The only time I've had a job that did all that, I had to do very little work and I had time on the side to either write, or start a business, or have fun, or spend time with friends. The times when I haven't is when I was working too hard, dealing with people I didn't like, getting my creativity crushed over and over, and so on. When you are in those situations, you need to plot out your exit strategy.

Your hands are not made to type out memos. Or put paper through fax machines. Or hold a phone up while you talk to people you dislike. One hundred years from now, your hands will rot like dust in your grave. You have to make wonderful use of those hands now. Kiss your hands so they can make magic.

One can argue, not everyone is entitled to have all of those needs satisfied at a job. That's true. But since we already know that the salary of a job won't make you happy, you can easily modify your lifestyle and work to at least satisfy more of your needs. And the more these needs are satisfied, the more you will create the conditions for true abundance to come into your life.

Your life is a house. Abundance is the roof. But the foundation and the plumbing need to be in there first or the roof will fall down and the house will be unlivable. You create the foundation by following the Daily Practice. I say this not because I am selling anything but because it worked for me every time my roof caved in. My house has been bombed, my home has been cold, and blistering winds have frostbitten my nerve endings, but I managed to rebuild. This is how I did it.

7) Your retirement plan is for shit. I don't care how much you set aside for your 401(k). It's over. The whole myth of savings is gone. Inflation will carve out the bulk of your 401(k). And in order to cash in on that retirement plan you have to live for a really long time doing stuff you don't like to do. And then suddenly you're eighty and you're living a reduced lifestyle in a cave and can barely keep warm at night.

The only real retirement plan is to Choose Yourself. To start a business or a platform or a lifestyle where you can put big chunks of money away.

Some people will say, "Well, I'm just not an entrepreneur."

This is not true. Everyone is an entrepreneur. The only skills you need to be an entrepreneur are the ability to fail, to have ideas, to sell those ideas, to execute on them, and to be persistent so even as you fail you learn and move onto the next adventure.

Be an entrepreneur at work. An "entre-ployee." Take control of who you report to, what you do, what you create. Or start a business on the side. Deliver some value—any value—to somebody, anybody, and watch that value compound into a career.

What is your other choice? To stay at a job where the boss is trying to keep you down, will eventually replace you, will pay you only enough for you to survive, will rotate between compliments and insults so you stay like a fish caught on the bait as he reels you in. Is that your best other choice? You and I have the same twenty-four hours each day. Is that how you will spend yours?

8) **Excuses.** "I'm too old." "I'm not creative." "I need the insurance." "I have to raise my kids." I was at a party once. A stunningly beautiful woman came up to me and said, "James, how are you!?"

WHAT? Who are you?

I said, "Hey! I'm doing well." But I had no idea who I was talking to. Why would this woman be talking to me? I was too ugly. It took me a few minutes of fake conversation to figure out who she was.

It turns out she was the frumpish-looking woman who had been fired six months earlier from the job we were at. She had cried as she packed up her cubicle when she was fired. She was out of shape, she looked about thirty years older than she was, and her life was going to go from bad to worse. Until...she realized that she was out of the zoo. In the George Lucas movie *THX-1138* (the name of the main character was "THX-1138"), everyone's choices are removed and they all live underground because above ground is "radioactive." Finally THX decides it's better to die above ground than to suffer forever underground where he wasn't allowed to love.

He wasn't free.

He makes his way above ground, evading all the guards and police. And when he gets there, it's sunny, everyone above ground is beautiful, and they are waiting for him with open arms and kisses. The excuse "But it's radioactive out there!" was just there to keep him down. [By the way, I've mentioned this example to people before and they usually reply, "Uh, that wasn't in the movie." Okay, you're right. Read the book!]

"This is easy for you to say," people say to me. "Some of us HAVE to do this!" The now-beautiful woman had to do it also. "What are you doing now?" I asked her. "Oh, you know," she said. "Consulting."

But some people say, "I can't just go out there and consult. What does that even mean?"

And to that I answer, "Okay, I agree with you." Who am I to argue? If someone insists they need to be in prison even though the door is unlocked, then I am not going to argue. They are free to stay in prison.

9) **It's okay to take baby steps.** "I can't just QUIT!" people say. "I have bills to pay." I get it. Nobody is saying quit today. Before a human being runs a marathon they learn to crawl, then take baby steps, then walk, then

run. Then exercise every day and stay healthy. Then run a marathon. Heck, what am I even talking about? I can't run more than two miles without collapsing in agony. I am a wimp.

Make the list right now. Every dream. I want to be a bestselling author. I want to reduce my material needs. I want to have freedom from many of the worries that I have succumbed to all my life. I want to be healthy. I want to help all of the people around me or the people who come into my life. I want everything I do to be a source of help to people. I want to only be around people I love, people who love me. I want to have time for myself.

THESE ARE NOT GOALS. These are themes. Every day, what do I need to do to practice those themes? It starts the moment I wake up. "Who can I help today?" I ask the darkness when I open my eyes. "Who would you have me help today?" I'm a secret agent and I'm waiting for my mission. Ready to receive. This is how you take baby steps. This is how eventually you run toward freedom.

10) **Abundance will never come from your job.** Only stepping out of the prison imposed on you from your factory will allow you to achieve abundance. You can't see it now. It's hard to see the gardens when you are locked in jail. Abundance only comes when you are moving along your themes. When you are truly enhancing the lives of the people around you.

When every day you wake up with that motive of enhancement. Enhance your family, your friends, your colleagues, your clients, potential customers, readers, people who you don't even know yet but you would like to know. Become a beacon of enhancement, and then when the night is gray, all of the boats will move toward you, bringing their bountiful riches.

This chapter is not a wake-up call. It's not a fear-mongering, "get ready to be poor" sort of chapter. It's not even a rallying cry to the greatness and plentitude of entrepreneurship. It's reality.

Let's Get Specific:
What Should I Do?

You're probably asking: well, if I quit my job, what should I do?

I've begun asking people who did it. What did they do? How do they quit their jobs and, basically, make a million dollars? Not everyone is Mark Zuckerberg or Larry Page. Not everyone is going to drop out of college and create an iPhone or a time machine or a toilet that resizes itself automatically depending on who is sitting on it (although that would be pretty cool).

Some people would simply like to quit their current crappy jobs and make a good living. Some people would simply like to quit their jobs and make a million dollars. In that Facebook movie (you know, the Justin Timberlake vehicle), JT says, "A million's not cool. A BILLION is cool."

Well, actually JT, very often a million is pretty cool. Not everyone is going to be a VC-funded $100 million hotshot. Sometimes it's nice to make a million dollars, be your own boss, and use that financial success to catapult to freedom.

I called Bryan Johnson, who started a company called Braintree. You may have never heard of Braintree but you've heard of their customers. They provide credit card transaction and payment services for companies like OpenTable, Uber, Airbnb, etc.

I've never spoken with Bryan before. I am not an investor in Braintree. As far as I know I'm not even an investor (unfortunately) in any of Braintree's clients. I like to call people who I think have interesting stories and hear what they have to say. That's the way I build my network of not only financial contacts but also potential friends.

I knew Bryan had an interesting story about how he set up Braintree and I knew it would be helpful for those people asking "what do I do next?"

The Cliff's Notes version: In 2007, Bryan was a manager at Sears. He quit his job and started Braintree. Within two years he was making more than a million per year. Eventually Braintree grew much bigger and raised $70 million from Accel and others investors.

But that wasn't what was interesting to me.

"How did you do it?" I asked him. "What are the steps?"

"I really disliked my job," he said, "and I never believed in the idea of getting a fixed wage. I had been a salesman before in the credit card processing business where I would go out and get merchants like restaurants and retailers to switch their business to the company I was selling for. So I figured I could do this but work for myself instead of another company."

Rule #1: Take out the middleman. Instead of going back to the company he used to sell for, Bryan cut out the middleman and went straight to a credit card processor, worked out his own reselling agreement with them, and did all of this BEFORE leaving his job at Sears.

Many people ask me, "I'm at a job, should I raise VC money yet?" NO, of course not! First you have to hustle. VCs want to back someone who shows a little Ooomph!

Rule #2: Pick a boring business. Everyone is always on the lookout for "the next big thing." The next big thing is finding rare earth minerals on Mars. That's HARD WORK. Don't do it! Bryan picked a business that every merchant in the world needs. He also knew that it was an exploding business because of the e-commerce explosion. You don't have to come up with the new, new thing. Just do the old, old thing slightly better than everyone else. And when you are nimble and smaller than the behemoths that are frozen inside bureaucracy, often you can offer better sales and better service. Customers will switch to you. If you can offer higher touch service as well, they will come running to you.

Rule #3: Get a customer! This is probably the most important rule for any entrepreneur. People want to find and take the "magical path": get VC money, quit their jobs, build a product, and then have millions of customers. It NEVER works like that.

Bryan found ten customers (out of the first 12 he approached) who would switch their credit card processing to him. He figured he needed to make $2100 a month to quit his job. With his first ten customers he was making $6200 a month, so he had a cushion in case some dropped away. He quit his job and suddenly he was in business.

Rule #4: Build trust while you sleep. This rule is often "Make Money While You Sleep." But Bryan was already making money while he slept. He was making money on every credit card purchase with his first ten customers.

"I didn't want to be going up and down the street looking for customers," Bryan said. "I needed to find a way to get online businesses as customers. Someone suggested that I needed to blog. And to blog well you need to be totally transparent or it won't work. So I started blogging about what was really happening in the credit card industry including all the unscrupulous practices and how merchants were being taken advantage of. Then I'd put my posts on the top social sites at the time--Digg, reddit, and StumbleUpon--and sometimes the posts would get to the top of these sites and my website would get so much traffic that it would crash.

"But I became a trusted source about credit card processing. So before long all these online sites that had previously had a hard time navigating this industry would start contacting me to switch their payment services."

A couple of things there.

Rule #5: Blogging is not about money. Blogging is about trust. You don't sell ads on your blog (rarely), you don't get the big book deal (rarely), but you do build trust and this leads to opportunities. My own blog has made me a total of zero cents but has created millions in opportunities. In Bryan's case it led to more inflow and his biggest early opportunity.

"Basically, OpenTable called me and they wanted a software solution to handle storing credit cards, handing the data to restaurants, and being compliant from a regulatory standpoint. I signed a three year deal with them that allowed me to build a team of developers and we built them a solution. We now had more services to sell to customers."

Rule #6: Say YES! He started out just connecting merchants with a credit card processor. Then OpenTable asked him to do software development even though he's never developed software before. He said YES! He got software developers, built a great product, and *at least* quadrupled his income. His decision to say YES! elevated his business to a whole new level, not just in the services he offered customers but in how they perceived him. Suddenly, word of mouth was spreading and other online companies started using Braintree's services: Airbnb, Uber, etc. And the VCs started calling because all of their clients were saying Braintree was providing all of their payment services. It's not that easy for startup online companies to get payment services.

Bryan told me, "When I first started, for each new customer we'd put together an entire package for our credit card processor on why we thought the customer could be trusted and would be a legitimate merchant." Which leads to…

Rule #7: Customer Service. You can treat each customer, new and old, like a real human being. "We intuitively sort of knew what we didn't like in customer service everywhere else: automated calling trees, slow response times, poor problem solving, etc. So we made sure there was as little friction as possible between the customer contacting us and actually getting their problem solved." When you are a small business, there's no excuse for having poor customer service. Your best new customers are your old customers, and the best way to touch your old customers is to provide quick help when they need it. Customer services is the most reliable touch point to keep selling your service to them.

"Ok," I said, "I have to ask. At what point were you making over seven figures?"

By Year 2, Bryan was making over a million dollars and the business was doubling every year. They couldn't hire fast enough.

In 2011, after four years in business, Braintree took in its first dime of investment capital--$34 million in a Series A funding round. Two years later, according to Crunchbase, they process over $8 billion in credit card transactions annually.

Not bad for someone who quit his job and just wanted to figure out a way to get his bills paid.

So what does this mean for you?

I get BS e-mails all the time. "Make a million dollars buying gold!" "Make a million dollars in real estate!" "Here are the secrets to making a million dollars, revealed this one time only!" Then I click on the link and it's all BS. Vague answers, some testimonials and then you have to buy a package. It's all BS.

The rest of this chapter is about brainstorming specific ways to make a million dollars, to do what Bryan Johnson did in less than two years. This is all just brainstorming mind you, and it comes from my personal experience and expertise, so there will be limitations on its scope. But it's a start. It's where I start when I want to come up with a new business idea. It's where you can start, too. *Note:* every idea I mention below is an idea I've seen someone pursue to make a million dollars are more. Am I recommending these methods? No. But, again, they are starting points for brainstorming.

A) Make a service business on whatever the cutting edge of the Internet is. Start with small businesses. In the '90s, you would've made a website business. Right now you can build an app or make a social media agency. Don't just set up Facebook fan pages for people. Get those people some fans. Set people up on twitter. Then get those people followers. Set businesses up on YouTube, Pinterest, Wanelo, etsy, Quora, Instagram, MailChimp. Every small business (a law firm, a dentist's office, a flower shop, etc.) should have a working knowledge of some, if not all, of these tools. Your new agency can give it to them.

How do you find clients? Go to the local businesses you use. Ask them what they need and what you can do. Take on the first few clients for free and then start charging a monthly fee. Put out a letter to them each week about what new things you can be doing. Don't forget: the best new customers are current customers.

If you are an employee somewhere, go to your current employer. Offer them your services. If they say yes, then try to quit your job, start a company, and offer the services again. Heck, make them an equity owner in the company because they gave you your start.

All we are trying to do is make ONE MILLION DOLLARS, remember? Once you have a few hundred thousand in revenues and you start hiring people, sell the business for $1 million. That's it. There will be plenty of buyers (local ad agencies, bigger ad agencies trying to consolidate, bigger social media firms, small public companies trying to break into the ad space).

You're always selling: selling your services, selling your customers' services (!) (this is the real, true secret for keeping customers by the way), and selling your company.

B) Introduce two people. Every company is for sale. Every company has a price. And there are many entrepreneurs trying to buy businesses. Not just entrepreneurs either, but businesses called "roll-ups," whose entire business is buying other businesses. These companies buy many mom-and-pop operations in different regions, combine them together, fire all of the back-office staff that are redundant, and now they are a national business with greater margins that can go public or get acquired.

Sometimes companies need help finding buyers. Sometimes companies need help getting in shape to meet buyers. Sometimes companies have no clue about what to do next once they meet a buyer. A lawyer supposedly helps, but not really. They just add layers of process and remove layers of profit.

It's hard to navigate getting acquired. If you can be somewhere in the middle, you can get paid. There are some regulations around getting paid for this service, but if you can figure them out and build a business around this idea, you can make $1 million easy.

C) Write a book. I have never made $1 million writing a book. But I have a number of friends who have made millions writing books or information products of some sort. This is a tricky area, so the key here is that you have to be legit. Don't write a book on a subject you know nothing about. Then you're just like one of those BS e-mail spammers, except a hundred times worse because what they do in six hundred words you do in sixty thousand. Instead, partner with someone who knows something and write about what they did.

D) Write a book, part II. Actually, I lied. I just realized I have made $1 million writing a book. My very first book *Trade Like a Hedge Fund*. The book itself didn't make me that much—maybe $50,000, give or take—but in 2004, I started getting speaking engagements with companies like Fidelity, Schwab, Profunds.

A few other institutions would pay up to $20,000 per talk. I've probably given well over a hundred talks based on that book over the past nine years. Plus I've written articles for them and had other opportunities because of that book. Remember: when you write a book, it's not all about book sales. Books give you credibility in your area of expertise or interest. Credibility gets you:

- **consulting** (Tim Ferriss has done this very well)
- **speaking** (the authors of *Freakonomics* have made a career out of this)
- **other media opportunities** (TV show, radio show, etc.)
- **other writing opportunities.** Most authors I know, even bestselling ones, don't make millions from their books. But then they get paid to write for big-paying magazines or corporations or whatever. These add up. And if they add up enough, you can outsource a lot of your writing to people whom you trust, as long as you triple-check their work. When I was writing finance articles in 2005, I was writing up to five articles A DAY with the help of a team of cheap labor (high school students) who knew more about stocks than just about any hedge fund manager I knew.
- **an e-mail list** you can sell other products to. I have never done this but several of my friends (see Ramit Sethi's book or John Mauldin's book) have done it very successfully

E) Financial Repair. I was just visiting a friend the other day who was renting a $5 million mansion in South Beach, Miami. I asked him, "Who owns this place?" He said, "Some guy who figured out a way to make the points on your driver's license go away." The house had seven bedrooms, eight bathrooms, a music studio, a boat docked right off the back porch, and a closet bigger than the typical New York City apartment, and came with a personal chef. She cooked us lunch.

We live in an economy where the media reminds us almost every day how the divide between rich and poor is getting greater and greater. Screw the media! The situation is what it is. Let's not complain about politics or economics. Let's actually help people with money issues. Here's where people need help:

- parking tickets (like above)

- student loans. There are a trillion dollars in student loans out there. A business helping young people navigate their way through this loophole-filled landscape is easily a million dollar business.

- credit repair

- rent-to-own. I am forever against buying houses but, for better or worse, some people want to own homes. Who am I to stop them? Since 2008, many of these people can no longer afford to buy a home. Banks refuse to give out loans. Remember my friend from "How to Disappear Completely and Never Be Found," who bought up all the homes databases and built his own rent-to-own homes database? He charges a subscription fee for the database. And guess what? People subscribe to it. So much so that he's expanded his rent-to-own model.

He just launched a rent-to-own laptop product. He bulk buys the laptops for $200 apiece and rents-to-own them out for $20 a week for a year. BAM! Huge margins. He started just a few months ago. He's bringing in $300,000 a month now, and can sell his business for at least several million dollars pretty much any time he wants. And, by the way, he didn't go to college.

If you're like a lot of people who are doing this for the first time, all these brainstorming ideas probably make your head swim a little bit and leave you with a lot of questions. Since I started writing and giving talks, I've heard them all:

So should I quit my job? I have a million ideas, which should I do first? Do I just need to be a better multitasker? What do I do if I have ideas but I'm a procrastinator? I'm too busy, I have a family, I don't have time, what do I do then?

I get it. I understand what you're going through, believe me. This is very hard. Those are very hard questions. And I have specific answers to each of them. Unfortunately my answers don't matter—and won't matter—until you start from the beginning and get back to basics.

When I was a kid, I was scared to death of my grandma. When she would come over, the first thing she would do is go to my room and scream at me if it was a mess. We started having to slip more cortisone into her mouthful of daily vitamins just to calm her down.

To prepare for her visits, I started cleaning my room. I could do it superfast. The reason was because all I was doing was sweeping everything under my bed. My room would look spotless but it was actually still a disgusting mess.

The same thing is true of most people's lives. I don't say that in a critical way. I just know it's true. Every time I lost money, it was because I had fooled myself into thinking I was in great shape, but there was still a lot of crap swept under the bed. There's no getting around it. Cleaning your room, cleaning the house where your freedom lives—the house you want to live in—takes time and effort. It requires you build the proper foundation, by getting back to basics.

The way you get back to basics is by doing your Daily Practice and focusing on the Four Bodies (do one from each, every day):

The Physical Body: Am I eating well? Am I exercising? Am I flossing? Am I sleeping enough? There are really no shortcuts. The only people I know who claim they sleep "three hours a day and still have a ton of energy" are 100 percent bipolar. No joke.

The Emotional Body: Am I surrounding myself with people who love me? Am I not engaging with the people who put me down, even if they are co-workers? Am I not gossiping? Am I expressing gratitude to the people who are good to me? I bet this seems corny, right? You're probably asking yourself, *what does this have to do with a million dollars?*

Last year, my friend from Miami (the one with the mansion) made several million dollars in his business. A few years ago, he was broke, living in his parents' basement. He was overweight and unhealthy. He was in a bad relationship. And his ideas were stale, left over from the last time he made a million (which he of course then lost).

What changed?

Like many people, he realized that he had to do something different in order to get out of the rut he was in. There's a saying, "It's your best thinking that got you here." So the first step is to literally throw away your "best thinking."

My friend realized that the first step was to get back to the basics. He simply began by jogging and eating better. That sense of self-improvement then started to extend out to his relationships, his creativity, his spiritual life, and all of this together transformed the way he thought about his business. It's not that his business got better. It's that his thinking got better because it came from a foundation of health. And from that foundation, you build the house you want to live in.

Now he's out of the bad relationship. He's lost fifty pounds. He has a personal chef who cooks only healthy meals for him. He hired someone to help him with the marketing of his business, which helped him to generate new, fresh ideas. And the arrogance that he was known for in his circle seems to be greatly tempered.

The Mental Body: People have lots of ideas, but they are mostly bad ones. The way you get good ideas is to do two things: 1) Read two hours a day. 2) Write ten ideas a day. By the end of a year, you will have read for almost one thousand hours and written down 3,600 ideas. One of these ideas will be a home run. How will you know which one? Or two? Or three? Well, because you are doing your Daily Practice and focusing equally on the other three bodies, which are essential for health.

The Spiritual Body: I was leading a retreat at a spiritual "resort" a few months ago. I wanted to charge nothing and title it "Creating Success from Within." Two things happened. The retreat center said, "No, you have to charge!" And then they said, "You can't use the word *success*. Our audience doesn't like that."

I thought this was funny. Spiritual people hate the word *success*, yet they are more than willing to charge their "audience" an arm and a leg to achieve it. FYI, I'm pretty sure that's called "a scam." Not that "success"-oriented people are any better. They hate the word *spiritual* just as much. It reminds them of New Age bullshit or their childhoods, when they were forced into boring, religious instruction by parents who needed the threat of eternal damnation in order to get their kids to clean their rooms.

So let's just move away from all that. Don't worry about satisfying anybody else's preconceived notion of what spirituality is. Some people say, "Oh! You have to meditate!" You have to sit in the lotus position! Blah blah blah.

No, you don't.

All you have to do is stay in the present. When you catch yourself upset about the past or worried about the future, say to yourself, "Ah, I'm time traveling," then STOP. That's what meditation is. That's what being "spiritual" means: *not* time traveling. Don't believe anyone who says it isn't. And you can practice it all day. Still unsure?

Do this every day: wake up and think of five people you are grateful for in your life *right now*. Not people who you *were* grateful for in the past. And not people you hope to be grateful for in the future if they do what you want them to do. Five people RIGHT NOW. That's all you have to do. Want to take it further? Surrender to the fact that you can't control ALL of the events in your life. Those people you hope to be grateful for probably aren't going to do exactly what you want them to. All you can do is the preparation. The food will taste how it will. Finally, try to label your thoughts: "future" or "past." If you can do that, you stand a pretty good chance of remaining in the present.

When you start to question and practice in these four areas—when you get all four of these bodies healthy—the quality of your ideas will get better, you will have more energy and time, and you will build the basic foundation that will later turn into the house you want to live in.

The global financial crisis was the only recession in history during which corporate cash actually went UP quarter over quarter every single quarter. The result is that there is a massive amount of money out there. Trillions of dollars. Meanwhile, millions of people went unemployed (or underemployed) and into financial stress. Is that you? Are you one of those millions in distress, in need of help, looking for your freedom? This chapter about specific choices was written specifically for you.

I'm not trying to throw crap on the wall here. I'm not trying to sell you anything. I'm not recommending any one of you try any one of the specific brainstorm ideas I laid out above. What I am trying to do though, is to get you to do *something*. Something that can increase your chances of making $1 million. Something specific that can get you healthy, and be the first concrete step on the path toward choosing yourself.

IT DOESN'T COST A LOT TO MAKE $1 BILLION

Nobody chooses themselves to make $1 billion. You don't wake up and say, "I'm going to do whatever it takes to make a lot of money." You wake up and you say, "I have a big problem. And a lot of people have the same problem. And nobody is going to solve this problem except for me."

Even better, can you say "A million people have this problem?"

Corporate America doesn't solve problems. These companies are machines that keep churning out the same product, with minor tweaks, forever.

With new technology, new methods of marketing, and a healthy, balanced life that helps you come up with ideas and execute on them, you can become the sort of person who solves problems that help millions of people.

It's the external manifestation of if you better yourself, you better the lives of the people around you.

Sara Blakely decided she had a problem. A big one. She wanted to look better when she wore panty hose.

Specifically, she didn't want the unsightly bulge that occurs at the end of panty hose underneath the skirt. She solved the problem by creating a seamless panty hose. You may have heard of it. It's called Spanx, Sounds easy? Sounds trivial? It is. Even she will admit it. And now she's worth $1 billion.

Am I glorifying the billion dollars? Sure I am. That's what people notice. Nobody cares about someone who made a new panty hose. But that's the problem she solved that led to everything else. She simply wanted to look better. And then her friends wanted to look better. And so on.

Here are my takeaways from Sara's story:

Stay motivated. She had been reading self-help books (specifically Wayne Dyer's earlier books) and motivational books since she was sixteen years old. What's a self-help book do? It tells you that part of the world around you exists because you "think" it to exist. Extreme example: if you are lying on the floor depressed all the time, you won't seize opportunities. If every day you wake up and say, "What adventure will happen to me today?" then adventures will happen to you. So from an early age she trained herself to look for the opportunities in life. She trained herself for ten years thinking that way before the idea for Spanx hit her. Without thinking about it, she was bringing about the Daily Practice in her life, from spirituality, to mental health, to emotional health, to physical health.

She was amazingly good at sales. Sara had to sell fax machines for Danka as one of her first jobs. Within a few years, by the time she was twenty-five, she was the national sales trainer. People shy away from the word *salesman*. They think the process of selling is "dirty" in some way. But the only way to get anywhere is to come up with ideas and then have a strong ability to sell them. Sara had that ability.

She solved a huge problem for women. If you want to create $1 billion in value, you need to find a problem that nobody has solved. Right now, this second, there are about 1 million problems that, if you solved one, someone else would say, "Holy shit! That's so easy. Why didn't I think of that?" And yet, these problems, right now, remain unsolved.

So what was the problem she "solved"? Ninety-nine percent of women complain about the "muffin top" that forms after the panty hose ends and their stomach takes over. No problem, said Sara, here's an idea for panty hose that solves it. They're panty hose that don't have feet and also smooth out a woman's body underneath her dress. Then she went out and did it. Now woman look sexier. Not only was this a huge problem for women, it solved a pretty big issue for men as well! We like looking at sexy women.

Prepare. How did she do it? Sara had never done anything in fashion before. So she spent every day at the library and the hosiery stores. She had a full-time job but at night she researched every patent. She bought every type of panty hose. She knew the entire industry. To succeed at something:

- Know every product in the industry
- Know every patent
- Try out all the products
- Understand how the products are made
- Make a product that YOU would use every single day. You can't sell it if you personally don't LOVE it

Cold-call. When I was trying to get people to use Stockpickr .com—a site I built from 2006 to 2007—I cold-called AOL, Yahoo, Google, Reuters, Forbes, etc. Guess what? Everyone responded, because I knew it was something they all needed. I had at least two to five meetings with each group and did deals of some sort or another with all of them. If you have something that's worthwhile, you can't be afraid to cold-call. They need you more than you need them.

What does this have to do with Sara Blakely and Spanx? She cold-called the number-one place to sell her stuff—Neiman Marcus—and they loved her product and took it right away.

AN ASIDE:

Someone asked me yesterday if I had any connections at a major children's company so she could sell an excellent set of children's travel books to them. I think it's a great idea. Why? Because I see my kids buy every book from this children's company. It's a doll company but they also put out books like, "How to be a child of divorce" as an example (which both my kids, being children of divorce, have read thoroughly). So why not travel books? This woman has already made a dozen travel books for kids ages eight to twelve, the exact age group for this children's doll company. I know she's a good writer because my kid even did a book report on one of her books and loved it. So I know kids would love her travel books.

She wanted a connection in because she was afraid to cold-call. But almost all sales are done through cold calling. If there's a need, people will love to meet you. Cold-call right now!

It doesn't cost much to make a billion. Sara started with $5,000. That's it. She never took investors. She never borrowed money. Now her revenues are hundreds of millions a year. Facebook spent a few thousand to get to the point where they had 1 million users a day. Google hardly spent any money at first. Not that I'm in the billion-dollar league, but I can tell you that Stockpickr.com cost me less than $5,000 to build and was sold for $10 million a few months later. And the first company I sold cost *less* than $0 to build. We had profitable clients from day one.

If you have an idea, don't focus on the money. Don't focus on how you will make a living. Do this:

- Build your product
- Sell it to a customer
- Start shipping
- **Then** quit your job.

Sara didn't quit her job until she was already well on her way to selling her first million in orders. Most entrepreneurs write me before they have a product even built. They have "an idea" and they want to quit their job to pursue it so they need to raise money right now. Are you crazy? Anyone who would give you money might as well get really good with a plunger because they are going to need it after the money gets flushed down the toilet.

Never ask permission, ask for forgiveness later. Sara didn't like how Spanx were being displayed at Neiman Marcus. So she bought samples of her own product at Target and displayed them right next to the cash register at Neiman Marcus. She knew innately that nobody would question her. Nobody questions anything if you have confidence, intelligence, and you are proud of your product. This is like the Stanley Milgram experiment mentioned in the chapter "And Then They All Laughed." You just ASK for the subway seat and people give it to you.

Sara just did it. To hell with the ramifications. What else did she do? She sent Spanx to Oprah Winfrey's stylist. Who was more perfect to wear Spanx than Oprah Winfrey?

Take advantage of all publicity. I'm bad at this. I say no to almost everything. CNBC used to call me all the time and I wouldn't even return their calls. Finally Jim Cramer said to me, "Why are you embarrassing me like this. Return their calls." He made the very good point that if you don't promote yourself, nobody else will.

I first heard about Spanx when Sara Blakely was on the Donnie Deutsch show. But *millions* heard about it through Oprah, an opportunity that Sara created for herself. She also spent a season on Richard Branson's reality show, defying every fear she ever had. She promoted herself down every avenue. That's what you have to do to succeed. You can't have any shame. I have a lot of shame in promoting myself, which I have to get over. She had no shame. Not to over-repeat a catchphrase, but Sara didn't wait for anyone to choose her. She chose herself in every way.

Looks. I'm not saying good looks or bad looks. But YOU are the best promoter of your product. So if your product is something in the fashion industry, you should make sure you are the best model for it. A good friend of mine is about to launch a skin cream for Latina women. The cream smooths out wrinkles and also smooths out the different shades of color on the face that many Latinas have. She's about forty years old. I can tell you this: she doesn't have a single wrinkle and her skin glows. She will be the best model for her product.

Remember, you don't have to be great looking. I'm a weird, geeky-looking guy. Who better to sell a website? Or website services in the '90s like I used to. If I looked like a J. Crew model, I might've failed. Instead, I had the look of a dirty computer genius (even though I was thrown out of computer science grad school) and I can tell you, that look worked for me.

Good for her. Don't be a hater! Ninety-nine percent of people are haters. Bless that which you want.

If you want to be successful, you need to study success, not hate it or be envious of it. **If you are envious, then you will distance yourself from success and make it that much harder to get there.** Never be jealous. Never think someone is "lucky." Luck is created by the prepared. Never think that someone is undeserving of the money they have. That only puts you one more step removed from the freedom you aspire to. I can tell right away that when someone is so envious and jealous, they will never get the freedom they want but will spend the rest of their life trying.

It's not about the money. Sara had to tell her fiancé a few weeks before their wedding that Spanx wasn't just selling a few million dollars' worth a year but hundreds of millions of dollars' worth a year.

That's a big difference, right? And it was only a few weeks before their wedding.

As he put it in a later interview: "She said to me, 'I'm not sure you really know how successful Spanx is—[and] I am.'" After she told him, her fiancé started crying. "I was just so happy for her." He had already sold a successful, private-plane rentals company to Berkshire Hathaway and wasn't doing badly himself. But it shows how little money played a role in how she defined herself.

In an interview with *Forbes* she said, "I feel like money makes you more of who you already are. If you're an asshole, you become a bigger asshole. If you're nice, you become nicer. Money is fun to make, fun to spend, and fun to give away."

In the past fifteen years, the only time I didn't look at my bank account every day was when I was doing something I was passionate about. Sara was clearly passionate about Spanx. The money quickly became an afterthought.

This doesn't mean you shouldn't think about money. But it does mean if YOU ARE thinking too much about money while building your business, then either you are not very passionate about the business or you aren't helping people with your business. Those two thoughts alone will crowd out the thoughts of your own personal bank account.

My final takeaway: god bless her. She's worth $1 billion.

BECOMING A MASTER SALESMAN

No amount of schooling will teach you how to choose yourself. I don't want to do an anti-school rant here. I've done that before. Let's focus on the things school doesn't teach you, because these are the exact things you need to survive: how to come up with ideas (discussed in an earlier chapter), how to sell those ideas, and how to fail and bounce back. Then repeat.

Someone I don't know at all just wrote me with the worst-selling technique of all time. He wrote, "I really need to talk to you. Can I have twenty to thirty minutes of your time?"

The answer is no. Not that I think I'm so great. Or that my time is so valuable. But his message sort of suggests that my time is worth zero. He is offering me nothing, even less than nothing since there's opportunity cost to twenty to thirty minutes of time. I could be watching half an episode of *Mad Men*, for instance. Or researching how to code Wifi into protein (not giving up on that one yet).

There are some variants on this horrible technique. Like, "I have a great idea that I'll give you equity in if you give me twenty to thirty minutes of your time." I don't know if his equity is worth anything yet, so it's the same problem as above.

Another sign of a bad salesman is a good negotiator. This might not always be true, but it's true for me. I am horrible at negotiation. If I say, "This car is for sale for $10,000" and they say, "Eight thousand," I shrug my shoulders and say, "Okay."

When you're negotiating you have to say no a lot. When you are selling, you are always trying to find the "yes."

Everyone has a "yes" buried inside of them. A good salesman knows how to find where that "yes" is buried and then how to tease it out. Great salesmen know it instinctively.

When you're a negotiator you have to be willing to say no, regardless of what the other side says.

So although they aren't total opposites, the goals are completely different.

Negotiation Is Worthless. Sales Are Everything.

Why? Because when someone says "yes" to you, you are in the door. Eventually then, you'll get the girl (or guy, whatever) in bed. If you negotiate right at the door, then you might have to walk away and try the next house. That takes time and energy, and still might not work out.

In fact, not only will "bad negotiation" often result in great sales (and frankly I'd rather be in the bed than walking door to door) but, if you are a master salesman, it will also lead to the best result.

Some examples of my "bad negotiation" style that have worked out for me:

A) I sold my first business for less than other Internet businesses were going for at the same time. It was 1998, the Internet was about to go bust, but first all the stocks went up. Maybe I sold too early. It certainly seemed that way for a while. But better to sell early than go broke. Some people say, "why not go for the long run—build a business that lasts forever. Very few businesses last forever. There's a reason it's called "fifteen minutes of fame." That doesn't apply to just people. It applies to almost everything.

B) I gave 50 percent of Stockpickr to thestreet.com for no money. Blogs were written about how bad my deal was. But when someone owns 50 percent of your business, they care about what happens. They had to buy my company four months later rather than risk someone else owning 50 percent of it. For companies they only owned 10 percent of, they gave up on them. I was able to sell about four months before the market peaked. After that, it never would've happened. My one employee quit on me because he was so disgusted with the deal I did. At the time it didn't seem like it was the best negotiation. In fact, it seemed like I was a horrible negotiator. And I am. But more important is to build relationships than to kill everyone and take every last dime in a negotiation.

C) I sold Claudia's car for $1,000 less than she wanted to sell it for. But now the car is gone. We don't have to worry about it. That was worth $1,000 to me. And we stopped paying $600 a month to park it in downtown New York City. That's +$1,600 in my book.

D) I got my old company to do websites for New Line Cinema for $1,000 a movie—which was one two-hundredth of what we got for doing *The Matrix* site—even though some of the sites were the same size as that site. Why did I do that? The best designers wanted us to hire them to work on those movies.

Meanwhile, they stayed late on Saturday nights to work on Con Edison sites that paid a lot better. I didn't negotiate at all.

E) I've sold my books on Kindle for almost nothing. I've given away books for free to people who showed up at my talks or signed up for my newsletter. Does that sound stupid? Maybe. But it got my name out there. I've now given out more than one hundred thousand copies of my books, on top of the sales. This will have lifelong effects for me. I feel them every day.

F) I get offers every day to advertise on my blog. I say no to every one of them. Monetizing my site? Not part of my big picture.

The key is, don't be stupid. Only negotiate with people you really want to sell to. Otherwise it boils down to just money. Creating value goes right out the window. And only sell something you love to someone you love. Always think, "What is the bigger picture here?" In many cases, in the bigger picture, the negotiation is not as important as the "sale." Who cares if you got yourself a great price on a product that no one's heard of or cares about? Hence, the rise of models like "freemium."

Ten keys to selling:

- A) **What's the lifetime value of the customer?** When I give away a book for free, it gets my name out there. That has lifelong value for me that goes way beyond the few dollars I could maybe charge. When you add value to people's lives (for instance, giving away quality content for free), the opportunities that come back to you cannot be quantified. I've had the strangest opportunities this past year because of the honesty I offer on my blog. Sometimes it's almost seemed like magic. But that's okay. I like being a magician.

B) **What are the ancillary benefits of having this customer?** When we did Miramax.com for $1,000, we became the GUYS THAT DID MIRAMAX.COM! That helped get twenty other customers that were worth a lot more. I would've paid Miramax money to do its site.

C) **Learn the entire history of your client, your audience, your readership, and your platform.** You need to love your client. Love all of their products. Infuse yourself with knowledge of their products. I wanted to work at HBO because I loved all of their shows, and I studied their history back to the '70s before I applied for a job there in the '90s.

D) **Give extra features.** Do the first project cheap. And whatever was in the spec, add at least two new cool features. This BLOWS AWAY the client. Don't forget the client is a human, not a company. That human has a boss. And that person wants to look good in front of her boss. If you give her a way to get promoted, then she will love you and always hire you back. Don't forget to always give extra. A simple effort will get you a customer for life.

E) **Give away the kitchen sink.** One of the biggest investors in my fund of hedge funds had just been ripped off in a Ponzi scheme. They almost went out of business. I introduced them to reporters at every newspaper to help them get the word out about the Ponzi scheme. They were infinitely grateful and even put more money in my fund. Whenever the main guy was depressed about what had happened, I would talk to him for an hour trying to cheer him up. I wasn't just a fund he invested in but a PR person and therapist. Go the extra mile.

F) Recommend your competition. Think about it this way: what are two of the most popular sites on the Internet? Yahoo! and Google. What do they do? They just link to their competition, other websites. If you become a reliable source, then everyone comes back to you; if your knowledge has value, they can only get that by having access to you. They get access by buying your product or services.

G) Idea machine. There's that phrase "always be closing." The way that's true is if you are always putting yourself in the shoes of your client and thinking of ways that can help them. When I sold Stockpickr.com to thestreet .com, the superficial reason was that they wanted the traffic, community, and ads my site generated. The real reason was that they needed help coming up with ideas for their company. I was always generating new ideas and talking to my contacts at thestreet.com about them. Often the real reason someone buys from you is not for your product, but for you.

H) Show up. When I wanted to manage some of Victor Niederhoffer's money[2], I read all his favorite books. I

---

[2] Victor Neiderhoffer is a famous hedge fund manager who used to work with George Soros. In his day, he was so good, Soros sent his son to work with Neiderhoffer to learn how to trade.

wrote articles for him. At the drop of a dime, I would show up for dinner wherever and whenever he asked me to. If he needed a study done that required some programming beyond what he or his staff was capable of doing, I would offer to do it and do it fast. Nobody was paying me, but ultimately he placed money with me (at ridiculously low fees, but I did not negotiate), which I was able to leverage into raising money from others. Plus, I really liked him. I thought he was an amazing person.

I) **Knowledge.** When I was building a trading business, I must've read more than two hundred books on trading and talked to another two hundred traders. No style of trading was off limits. This helped me not only build a trading business, but build a fund of hedge funds, and ultimately build stockpickr.com. I felt like I knew more about trading and the top investors out there than anyone else in the world. Creating value was almost an afterthought. When I was building websites, I knew everything about programming for the web. There was nothing I couldn't do. And the competition, usually run by businessmen and not programmers, knew that about me. And they knew that I would always come in cheaper.

J) **Love it.** You can only make money doing what you love. If you work a 9 to 5 job that you hate, then you're on a leash that gives you just enough lead to get by and stops just short of real freedom and happiness. And money. If you love something, you'll get the knowledge, you'll get the contacts, you'll build the site with the features nobody else has, you'll scare the competition, and you'll wow the customers.

I didn't enjoy writing finance articles. I'd write a finance article for some random finance site and then repost it on jamesaltucher.com. I had zero traffic. Then I decided to write articles I enjoyed. To get back to my true roots, where I loved writing and reading. I also wanted to really explore all of my failures, my miseries, and my pain. In public. I love being honest and intimate with people. I love building community. I love e-mailing with readers. It was about a little over a year ago that I decided to make the shift where I was just going to open the kimono at jamesaltucher.com and say everything I wanted to say, and at the same time indulge in my love of writing, art, creativity, and reading. More than 4 million "customers" later, I'm enjoying more than ever doing what I love.

How to Become an
Idea Machine

The Mental Body is the third leg of the Daily Practice. It is no more or less important than the other three legs. But many people get stuck here. They sit down with a pad and wait for God to come down and give them ideas to put on that pad. Or they wait for inspiration. Inspiration doesn't really exist.

Stephen King, in his book *On Writing* discusses an accident he once had that prevented him from writing for several weeks. When he started to write again he could feel the difference. He said how the words just weren't connecting right. His writing muscle had atrophied. He needed to exercise it again in order to continue writing the nonstop, bestselling thrillers he'd been writing for thirty years.

STEPHEN KING!

All it took was a few weeks out of action to throw him completely off his game even though he's one of the best in the world at what he does.

The idea muscle is no different than the writing muscle. It's no different than your leg muscles, for that matter. If you don't walk for two weeks, the muscles will atrophy. And you will need physical therapy in order to walk again.

The idea muscle must be exercised every day. Even if you've come up with ideas every day of your life, it will atrophy if you give it a two-week rest.

What are the benefits of having a functional idea muscle? You will become an idea machine. No matter what situation you are in, what problem you see in front of you, what problems your friends and colleagues have, you will have nonstop solutions for them. And when your idea muscle is at its peak performance, your ideas will actually be good, which again means you will be able to create the life you want to lead.

To become an idea machine takes about six to twelve months of daily practice with the idea muscle. Below I discuss how to develop that practice. And again, this goes side by side with the other three "bodies." You can't develop the idea muscle if you're suffering through a bad relationship, or an illness, or you lose your sense of gratitude and wonder toward the world around you.

In the mid-'90s, I had an idea that lasted about the amount of time it takes to drink two beers. I say this because I had the idea at a bar and it was quickly squashed by the two friends I was with.

I wanted to create a reality cable channel. All reality TV all the time. Reality TV was just beginning. MTV's *The Real World* and HBO's *Taxicab Confessions* were the only two real successful examples at that point. The day before, I had gone to a seminar at the Museum of Television and Radio about *The Real World*. All of the houseguests from my favorite season (but not Puck, or Pedro, who was dead) were there answering questions. I felt reality TV was a cheap way to produce TV and that people would get obsessed by it, particularly if sex was involved.

"What a dumb idea," a friend said. "There's only so much reality." Which strikes me as funny now.

The other guy said, "You're not a big TV company. How will you get the cable companies to go for the idea?"

So I never thought about it again. I put up a fence around the idea and decided I would never be able to leap over that fence to execute on the idea. Now EVERY television channel is basically all reality all the time, or at least 50 percent of the time.

My real problem was *I didn't have confidence*. And I didn't know what the next step was. In retrospect, I should've written down my idea, written down ten ideas for possible shows to launch with, and started pitching TV companies to get someone to partner with me on it. That would've been simple and not taken too much time before there was some payoff.

Note: what might be too big for you (thinking of the next step) might not be too big for someone else. They might easily know, and not be afraid of, what the next step is.

Two examples. Someone asked me, "How do you know when an idea is too big?" I answered that an idea is too big if you can't think of the next step. I then added that if I wanted to start an airline with more comfortable seats and Internet access and better food and cheaper prices, I might have a hard time because even if it were a good idea I wouldn't know what to do next.

Then I read about Richard Branson.

When Virgin Records was making him a tidy profit of about $15 million a year, he decided there should be a more comfortable transatlantic airline. What the hell did he know about making an airline? Nothing. Not only that, airlines are a difficult business. Three of the best investors in history, Howard Hughes, Carl Icahn, and Warren Buffett, have crashed and burned buying airlines. Warren Buffett once said something like "The best way to make a million dollars is to start with a billion and buy an airline. "

And yet Branson came up with the idea and that very day he called up Boeing to find out what it would cost to lease an airplane. He made a great deal with them that if it didn't work out he could return the airplane. If it *did* work out, he'd be a great customer for them. I'm assuming he made a similar call to Airbus and took the best deal. He then probably found out what it cost to lease space in the various airports he would need to use. They were probably happy with more business. And then, I'm guessing, he hired some pilots, some ground crew, and put an ad in the paper advertising his new air routes and he was in business.

Virgin Air is successful (I just flew it from New York to LA a few weeks ago), and has since spun off Virgin Galactic. So this scruffy kid, who started a record label, decided he wanted planes with more comfortable seats and is now, as a result, sending rocket ships into space.

Note the important thing: the day he came up with the idea, he also called Boeing and got a plane from them. Not only did he identify the next step, but he took it. For me, I would've convinced myself that the "next step" in starting an airline was probably too big for me. And then it *definitely* would've been too big for me. This is not quite the same as "the secret"—the idea that our thoughts can create our reality—but it's close. Our thoughts can make our ideal reality possible. If you think you can do something, if you have confidence, if you have creativity (developed by building up your idea muscle), the big ideas become smaller and smaller. Until there is no idea too big. Nothing you can't at least attempt. As Henry Ford said, "Whether you think you can, or you can't—either way you are right."

On a much smaller scale, I can state a few examples of my own but I'll stick with one. I had an idea to create a financial news site that didn't have any news but was just a site made up of various methods to come up with investment ideas. In particular, by piggybacking on the investment ideas of the greatest investors. I specced out the site on the morning I had the idea, I put the spec on elance.com, several developers contacted me with prices, and I hired one of them. Within a few weeks, version 1.0 of the site was released, stockpickr.com. Seven months and millions of unique users later, I sold the profitable company to thestreet.com.

So the question is not, when is an idea too big? It's how do I make all ideas smaller and achievable? You do this by developing the idea muscle:

Every day, read/skim chapters from books on at least four different topics. This morning I read from a biography of Mick Jagger; I read a chapter from *Regenesis*, a book on advances in genetic engineering, a topic I know nothing about. I read a chapter in *Tiny Beautiful Things* by Cheryl Strayed. Her other recent book, *Wild*, is an Oprah pick and was also excellent. I read a chapter from *Myths to Live By* by Joseph Campbell, and also, to waste time, I played a game of chess online.

Write down ten ideas. About anything. It doesn't matter if they are business ideas, book ideas, ideas for surprising your spouse in bed, ideas for what you should do if you are arrested for shoplifting, ideas for how to make a better tennis racquet, anything you want. The key is that it has to be ten or more.

You want your brain to sweat, like I mentioned earlier in the book.

Want to really sweat, and learn from my early mistakes with reality TV? Right now, list ten ideas that are "too big for me" and what the next steps might be. For instance, one idea might be "launch solar panels into outer space to more efficiently generate solar power." Another idea might be, "genetically engineer a microbe that sucks the salt out of water." I have no idea if that's even possible. Another idea might be, "within one year I am going to write a book and give away a million copies for free."

The first step would be to write the book. Then maybe I can crowd fund on kickstarter to give the book away for free. OR, I can maybe print up nano-size copies of the book so that you can only read it with a microscope but it would only cost me a couple of sheets of paper to print up a million copies. And so on. With the solar panels, I can call up SpaceX and see how much it would cost to rent space. For the microbe that desalinates…I have no idea. Can you help me?

You don't ever have to look at these ideas again. The purpose is not to come up with a good idea. The purpose is to have thousands of ideas over time. To develop the idea muscle and turn it into a machine.

Be a transmitter. Two farmers live side by side and drink their water from wells they've each built on their respective property. One farmer's well runs out of water and he needs rain to come quickly or he will die of thirst. The other farmer did the work and dug his well so an underground stream ran right into it. His well was always filled with water and he never had to worry.

How do you find and tap this underground stream?

By making sure the other parts of your life are in balance: you have no bad emotional situations/relationships happening or you are doing your best to stay disengaged from them. You are keeping physically healthy, limiting (or eliminating) alcohol, eating well, and sleeping well. And spiritually (a word I hate because of two hundred years of meaningless connotations that have been applied to it but I can't think of a better word), you realize that you can't control everything in your life, cultivating a sense of surrender to the present moment as opposed to time traveling to your regrets from the past and your fears of the future.

Activate another part of your brain. I write every day. Sometimes I need to reenergize other parts of my brain, to spark fires where things have gone dark. The other day Claudia and I took a watercolor class. I haven't done watercolors in my life. We got there and the next thing I knew it was three hours later. My brain didn't even notice the time passing. What did I have to show for it? The worst excuse for a sunset, some mountains, some clouds, ever done in watercolor. But my brain felt good.

Collisions. Ideas mate with other ideas to produce idea children. Read other ideas. Compare your new ideas with your old ideas. After the Big Bang, the rest of the universe was basically created from collisions. Hydrogen atoms collided to form helium atoms, and on and on until all of the elements were created. Dead stars collided with asteroids to create planets and water and ultimately life.

Collisions are the fundamental life-giving processes of the universe. Ideas are no different. The best ideas come from collisions between newer and older ideas.

Don't pressure yourself. This is similar to the "burnout" issue from the chapter "How to Choose Yourself." Sometimes you plant seeds but not every seed takes and grows into a beautiful plant. In fact, very few do. If you pressure yourself to turn every seed into the most amazingly beautiful plant the world has ever seen, then you are going to set yourself up for burnout and disappointment. You've consciously done all you can, now you need to let those unseen life forces go to work on the seeds. The best ones *will* sprout if you let them.

Shake things up. I have a very strict routine every day. I wake up, read, write, exercise, eat, attend meetings (phone or live), then reverse the process: eat, write, read, and sleep. Some days I have to work on something that's just not coming. And in those instances, I need to rejuvenate a little bit and shake things up. Do something different. Maybe I take a walk at 5 a.m. instead of reading. Maybe I sleep in four-hour shifts one day instead of eight hours straight. Maybe I spend a day writing handwritten letters instead of going on the computer. And when it comes to the work, it's enough to just jot down some ideas, or look at what I've done so far, and then set it down again. Get my subconscious working on it.

Shaking things up makes the brain say, "What the hell just happened?" And while the conscious brain is confused, the subconscious slips in and drops off what it's been working on while your conscious brain has been too busy. This is why so many people have ideas and "lightbulb" moments in the shower or when they are just about to fall asleep for a nap.

▶ An exercise to get your subconscious working on an idea: Write down your routine. Make it as detailed as possible. What can you change today? How can you change it?

List your childhood passions. When I was six years old, I was passionately interested in both comic books and Greek mythology. In high school and college, I took five years of French and spent some time in France (even had an office there with my first business). Right now I can't remember a single word of French except for maybe *oui*. But I remember vividly almost every comic and book I read about Greek myths from when I was six—from the very first comic (the "legion of superheroes" had to go back in time and stay with Clark's parents in Smallville) to every comic afterward.

We only ever remember the things we are passionate about. Ultimately, these become the fields where ideas bloom and are harvested. Everything else dries up inside and dies.

Try to think back to all the things you were ever passionate about from the age of five on. You'll be surprised how many things there were. And how many ways these passions can now be cross-fertilized and mate with each other to provide your next set of passions and ideas.

Surf the Internet. I just saw an "infographic" (infographics are quickly becoming the new blog posts) on how to be creative. It essentially read "Turn off the computer." Sometimes this is true. Sometimes not. With the entire world of knowledge at our fingertips, it sometimes is fun to get sucked down the rabbit hole like Alice and drift around in Wonderland. Some good places to start are brainpickings.org, thebrowser.com, and (not safe for work), extragoodshit.phlap.net. I might not get any ideas from what I see, but seeds might be planted. I find that I get a similar feeling when I go into the bookstore at a museum, pick out a bunch of books, sit down, and skim through them. It tickles the brain and lights things up that may have been dormant.

I asked people to help me come up with more ideas for coming up with ideas. Here are some of the suggestions people came up with. My thanks to all of these contributors:

Ben Nesvig
Three things I do when struggling for idea topics:

1. Twitter Search
I'll search phrases like:
"I wish I had"
"I just paid someone to"
"is the worst product"
"is a horrible company"
"has a terrible website"
"is my favorite website"
"does anyone know how"
With all of those terms, I'll think of ideas on how I could fulfill their wants or how that terrible website or company could be a little less terrible.

2. Groupon
A lot of companies that use Groupons are struggling for customers and need creative ideas. I'll take a look at the Groupon offers for that day and see if I can come up with other ways to promote the company or make their product better.

3. Hyper Focus/Freewrite

By default, everyone gives the minimum amount of attention required to complete tasks. To get ideas/insights/observations, I hyper focus. I'll set a timer for twenty-five minutes and focus and freewrite on one single thing. That usually brings up ideas I would have never thought about.

Pat P

Idea #10: I like to go to YouTube and put in a word relating to something I know nothing about or that I just happen to be interested in at that time and would like to know more. Then I watch a video on that subject. The risk is you waste some time watching a crappy video... the upside is unlimited. After a while your curatorial instincts get better and you know which ones from the many on any subject that YT serves up will be better than others. YT, like so much of the Internet, is an absolute treasure trove of info on nearly every subject and that, in itself, is the kernel of idea generation and mind-muscle exercise.

Kevin Faul

Find someone you don't know who interests and inspires you, then figure out how to reach them. Send them a kind note on LinkedIn or Facebook. Hit them up on Twitter. But research them first. I guarantee a quick conversation or e-mail exchange with someone inspirational will also inspire you. "Touching" someone who has made the impossible possible helps you realize that your ideas are also possible and inspire you to do more. Don't underestimate the power of being social.

The idea muscle is a natural side effect of putting the Daily Practice to work. When you are physically healthy, when you are around the people you love, when you exercise your idea muscle, and when you cultivate an ability to surrender to the reality around you, it frees you up so you can become an Idea Machine.

Everywhere you go, everything you see, every problem you confront, you will instantly be able to react to every situation that stands in your path. You will be like Spiderman with his spider sense that instantly reacts and knows what to do even before the problem surfaces. You don't have to believe me on this. I am only saying that this has worked for me and helped me to find great success. Try it for yourself and see. Maybe it will work for you, too.

Ten Ideas to Start You Off

I've given several talks and workshops where I handed out waiter pads and asked people to start writing down ideas. Sometimes people get a little anxious. So I give them a couple of guidelines.

1. **Write down as many ideas as you can.** You can't ask people for just one idea. They get very nervous because that one idea has to be the BEST idea.

2. **Share and combine ideas.** I call it having "idea sex" with each other. After they've written down their ideas, everyone picks a partner and they combine ideas.

Some of the results have been amazing. At one workshop, I asked people to come up with book titles, then combine their book titles with a partner and come up with a table of contents for the first book title on their combined list. I have yet to hear of a book from the people who went through this process that I didn't instantly want to read.

But the reality is, most ideas are bad. Most of my ideas are bad. I want you to feel comfortable coming up with hundreds of bad ideas. After I wrote the "How to Become an Idea Machine" chapter, I decided to come up with a list of ideas, a list that could help at least a million people. The key to ideas like this is to make sure you know what the next step is: e.g., you can't just say, "A time machine" unless you can actually spec out a time machine, which personally I am incapable of doing. So that idea is not on the list.

"Help a million people" is not a mandatory requirement for an idea list. It's just the idea list I'm going to create today. Having that criterion avoids genius ideas like "Lindsay Lohan plays Princess Leia's daughter in the next *Star Wars* movie." Admittedly (take note, J.J. Abrams), that is one of the best ideas anyone has ever heard. But it won't really help a million people. (Hmmm, I have to think about this for a second...no, no, it won't help a million people).

Feel free to steal any of these ideas. If you want to give me a cut, that's fine also.

A) I wrote down an idea here but I deleted it. It was simply too embarrassingly bad. I'm not afraid to admit when ideas are bad. More on this later.

B) Klout as currency. Think about it. It makes sense. If I give $5 to a donut shop, that means a lot less than if Barack Obama gives $5 to a donut shop. If Barack Obama buys a donut for $5 then that donut shop is the "Presidential Donut Shop." B's $5 is a lot more valuable than my $5. The $5 is just paper after all. It doesn't matter who holds it. Klout plus currency equals value in today's world. So it makes complete sense that people with higher Klout should be able to buy more things, because their currency is more valuable than mine. And when they buy things that infers Klout to the seller, who can either buy more things now, or even sell services at more expensive prices. This creates a natural social pricing mechanism around goods and services.

The world is heading in this direction anyway. Look at Oprah. Oprah has an infinite Klout score. If she bought a pencil from me, my Klout score would go up 80 percent, give or take. The middle class is disappearing. The temp staffers pay for goods with scrip, and rich people buy Twitter followers. We're moving toward a Klout-currency world anyway. Making it actually happen will encourage companies to create bigger value for their customers so that the value of their profits will go up, causing them to hire more people, etc.—a virtuous cycle.

C) Cryogenics for depressed people. Sometimes I know that in "the long run" things will work out. But I get scared about the short run. Another thing we all know is that time heals all wounds. But how much time does that mean? It differs per person. Let's say I get wounded. Metaphorically. Someone shoots me down and I feel bad. I might need a day or two to get over it. No problem, I step into my cryogenic tank and program it to wake me in a day. Or if I lose a loved one. That might take a year or two. Freeze me and wake me up on my birthday. Then I can look around, see how I feel, and go back under again. By the way, I don't age at all while I'm frozen, because all of my genes and chromosomes are at absolute zero. Sometimes it's financial. I might make an investment that will pay off in five years but I have little money now. No problem. Wake me in five years. Wake me when Twitter goes public.

D) Use global warming to solve global warming. I don't know why nobody has thought of this yet. Just look at the words *global* *warming*. The surface of the planet is getting hotter. That means it's giving off energy. Use photovoltaic strips (you like that?) to harness the energy coming off the planet to reduce our need for carbon-based energy. BAM! Problem solved. The beauty of this is that if there is no global warming, then the technique won't work. No problem! Go back to carbon then until the planet starts heating again. I used to go out with someone who worked on Al Gore's campaign. Hey, A*, if you read this and if you still have any feelings for me will you please contact him about my idea. He has a $10 billion fund, give or take, that he lives off of and he can really help me out here.

E) 3-D printing of humans. 3-D printing seems to be the latest tech fad. But whatever. I don't even know how it works. But here's what "3D Human Printing" is. Let's say I can't make a meeting tomorrow that's in India, eight thousand miles away. But I really want to go. I get in my suit at home and turn it on. In the conference room in Bangalore, another suit opens up. It opens its eyes. On the video screen in my suit I see what those eyes see. I move my arms and that suit moves its arms. I talk and that suit talks with my voice. Video conferencing can never replace face-to-face meetings. And even though this is sort of like advanced video conferencing, the minds of the other people in the room are basically psychologically fooled into thinking I am right there with them. It's just like if you take a robot and give it a human body, many people think it's almost like an actual human even though it's just a computer. This is one idea I can invent personally. And I have motivation. I don't like to travel. I like to sit at home and do nothing. With this invention I can travel all over the world. I can even go to Easter Island. This is sort of like Teleportation 101.

F) Advertising in houses. This sounds ugly at first: an ad on a wall in your house? Maybe in a frame like a picture. Or a mirror. But here's the deal: I get the price of my house reduced if I agree to allow advertising all over the house. Like if I'm sitting in the bathroom and I see "daily deals" projected onto the shower curtain. The ad agencies agree to subsidize part of the price of my house. It gets better. As part of this, they have software that listens to all my phone calls. Forget "social media." Let's see what I'm interested in when I'm ACTUALLY being social, e.g., talking to people on the phone. If I say on the phone, "I'd really love to go skiing this year but I can't afford it," I start getting offers for skiing trips at a discount on my shower curtain. It's win-win-win. I make money while talking to my friends. My house is cheaper. And companies sell more, improving the economy, hiring more people, and life goes from "bad" to "good."

G) Happiness hotspots. For ten years I've been getting business proposals like "with our product you will get alerted when your friends are close by." I actually think now is the time this will actually work because of the rise of phablets like the Galaxy Note. But forget that. When I want to see my friends, I'm not an idiot. I just call my friends and say, "Hey, let's meet for coffee." But let's make this localization thing really life-improving. Studies show that it's better to be around positive people than negative people. Positive people uplift you, negative people bring you down. So let's do this. Everyone wears an earplug that takes constant scans of your brain activity. The brain scans are matched against a database of ten thousand brain scans labeled "happy" or "sad," and then use standard speech recognition techniques to classify the user brain scan as either "happy" or "sad."

NOW, on my Google Maps on my phone I can see shades all over the map. The brightest colors denote areas where the happiest people seem to be. The darker colors denote areas where negative people are. So if I'm trying to decide today, "Hmmm, uptown or downtown?" I can look at the Happiness Map to see where the happiest areas are and go there. Who cares if my friends are there or not? I'll make new friends in the happy hotspots!

H) Forty percent unemployment. The reality is, most people should not be at work. Why? Other than the many reasons already elucidated in this book, it's simply because most people are bad at their jobs. It's rare that someone is actually good at what they do. I know maybe ten people who are good at their jobs. This is not a criticism. It's just a fact. And basically, robots are better. That's why Apple is moving production back to the United States, because too many Chinese people were killing themselves in their factories. Robots don't kill themselves, and they get the job done faster.

So what society really needs is 40 or 50 percent unemployment. Here's how you do it. My solution starts off communist but ends up libertarian. Basically, companies get incentivized to replace all humans with robots. The excess profits you get from firing people gets taxed at only half the rate. All of those "robot taxes" get put into a government fund that is used to subsidize the people who are fired (just like farmers are often paid subsidies not to farm). The subsidies, though, run out after three years. So you have three years from the day you are fired to start a new business. Hopefully the business uses robots instead of humans or else you won't be able to compete against your higher-margin competitors. If you can't start a business, then you end up being a temp staffer somewhere. Don't say this is heartless. This is the way the world is going. That's why the middle class is disappearing. Robots are the new middle class. And everyone else will either be an entrepreneur or a temp staffer. Don't shoot the messenger here. It's already happening. I'm just trying to figure out a way that we can actually accept the 40 percent unemployment or "underemployment" (already at 20 percent) that is coming.

I) Brain dating. This is a slightly different take on "G" above. No dating service works. The divorce rate is going up. Many people are not happy and end up cheating. A friend of mine recently got his results back from 23andme.com, which takes your spit and tells you everything you didn't know about yourself or things maybe you knew but forgot, like how old you were when you first experienced shame. I just sent my spit in two days ago and the day after they sent me a note telling me the price had gone down from $299 to $99. So I got screwed again by life but do I regret it? Of course not. That's the way I roll.

My friend got his results back and I asked him what the biggest thing he learned was. And he said, "That my father is my real father." He said, "A surprisingly large number of people are finding out that their biological fathers are not their real fathers." Why? Because people make mistakes. They get into relationships that are confusing, and they use confusing solutions to get out of them. Or even worse, they have babies.

So let's solve this and end a lot of misery. Take the brain scans of a thousand couples who are happily married after forty years. You know, the couples who say, "Well, we've had our problems but we've survived." Get rid of them. NO PROBLEMS. They are out there. Just a thousand couples of the 2 billion couples on the planet. Now average the brain scans together.

When you sign up for the brain dating service, you have to submit your brain scan. It averages your brain scan with the brain scans of all the women in the database. Then it matches the results against the database of one thousand happily married people. Whichever combination for you results in the closest match to those thousand brain scans, you get set up on a date with. Price: $10,000. The technology is there, people. Why aren't you entrepreneurs on top of this already?

J) A "Like" button in my contact lenses. I just read they are making contact lenses that can read texts. That's nice. I like to be in constant communication with everyone I know all the time. But let's take it one step further. I meet you, I like you, BAM, I blink twice quickly and my contact lens registers the like. Now you go about your day and other people who meet you can immediately see, "James has 158 Likes today." If you're having a bad day maybe you have only five "Likes." No problem. People will avoid you on those days and give you your space. Life is stressful and maybe you need a break. Tomorrow you might be refreshed and get more Likes again. I don't want just "social media." I want social LIFE.

Before I get to "K," I want to explain about "A." The original idea was "Wi-Fi with protein." When nomad tribes got to a new area fifteen thousand years ago they would think, "Where's the food?" Now, in my nomadic wanderings (i.e., New York City Starbucks locations) I think, "Where is the Wi-Fi?" Wi-Fi has clearly replaced food in our minds. So Wi-Fi with protein would solve the problem, right? But here's the issue. For the life of me, I can't figure out how you would do it. With every idea above

I can think of the next step. Ideas are a dime a dozen. It's all about EXECUTION. I just looked up everything I could about molecular biology on Wikipedia and I simply cannot figure out how to make Wi-Fi with protein. So I deleted that idea. No good. By the way, if you are Ridley Scott, please call me about licensing any of these ideas for a science fiction movie.

K) I don't have a "K". My brain is hurting. You might say I'm a dreamer. Or something like that. But if you can come up with a good "K" to help me round this out into ten ideas I'd be really grateful, and if I ever make a company out of it that makes a few billion dollars I'll give you a small piece of the company and part of my Klout score. Please follow me on Twitter so my Klout score goes up. I love you.

DON'T HAVE OPINIONS

Do you really think you are going to change anyone's mind? I always wonder, who are these people who spend all day on Internet message boards and comments sections getting really angry and trying to prove that their opinion is THE opinion that everyone should have.

And yet, we all get sucked in. Some anonymous teenager from Dubai might throw out an opinion that rubs us the wrong way and the next thing we know it's forty-eight hours later and we are in a drugged-out daze having spent the entire time peeing in a bottle and arguing in vain with this Internet troll. I wish I could say now, "So I went out and interviewed eighty-seven trolls and here is what they are really like." But I didn't. Because the trolls disappear. There are 7 billion people on the planet. The guy who disagreed with you is one of them. Good luck finding him.

What is the purpose of an opinion? To prove you're right? You're wrong.

Sometimes I get sucked in. Sometimes I write an article and people start saying the vilest things. I have no idea who they are, or even what their problems are, and yet I feel compelled to respond. I get sucked in. I feel so horrible about what they are saying. And when I finally come up for air, it's three days later and I think to myself, "what the hell have I just done."

I'm trying to eliminate things. Not just material belongings I no longer need or never really needed to begin with, but all those things we've been taught from birth are "important" or "our way of life" that have actually become burdens and wastes of time because we cling to them and protect them like they are more precious than the time and energy we waste protecting them.

Opinions are a way of clinging to the past. To some belief system our parents instilled in us, our education system "taught" us, our corporate masters forced on us, our peer group shoved down our throats, or some other brainwashing/programming that was implanted into our brain. If I have an opinion, you can gladly take it from me. Here's why:

A) Nobody is ever going to change his mind. For instance, if I say something like "kids shouldn't go to college," everyone either already agrees with me or disagrees with me. Very few minds will be changed no matter how correct I am (and I am correct). Here are some of my other opinions: buying a home is ALWAYS bad. Voting is stupid. Shakespeare is Boring. ZERO wars have been justified. Wyoming, North Dakota, and Montana should be handed over to the Jews and they should move from Israel to the United States. There! Go argue with that one.

B) One hundred years from now, everyone reading this book will be dead. I know there is a lab-coat army working in *Science* trying to change this. But, trust me, it won't work.

Science has its limits. And after seeing the shit you eat, don't count on being alive fifty years from now, let alone a hundred.

A year or so ago, a guy I didn't like died. We used to argue all the time over our opinions. Now he's dead. I guess I won. After he died it was amazing how many people wrote long, gushing tributes to him. One guy who told me that he was sexually harassed by the dead person wrote the most gushing one of all. Maybe they ended up having sex and it was wonderful. I don't know. I have no opinion on that one.

Which brings me to the more important issue: what if we argue and then you die? What if you have a heart attack while you are arguing with me? Is it my fault then? I don't want that kind of guilt on my conscience.

C) Us versus Them. The World Wide Web ("triple dub" for those in the business) has created this oozing lava of "Us" versus "Them." What happened before there were message boards? Before there were "threads"? Or hypertext?

Whenever some guy says something very hateful I imagine: what was it like the first time that person kissed his wife? Did a warm gush of chocolate fill his heart? Did he say to himself, "This second, I am the happiest man alive?" Did he have an erection? Did she kiss him softly on his lips and then his cheek and then his neck? And then, erection intact, did he log onto the Internet as "Guest" and post, "James Altucher is a fucking douchebag."?

D) Why educate people? In poker you can spot the amateur at the table if they complain when they lose a hand. They'll look at the guy who won the hand and say, "You are so stupid! You played that hand totally wrong. You just got lucky." And they might be right. But the reason that it's an amateur (and insecure) move is because you WANT people to play the hand wrong. You want them to play the hand wrong every single time so that the odds stay in your favor if you don't go insane. What do you gain from calling them out, educating them on their foolishness?

Only worry about your own happiness, which doesn't have to be limited by anyone else's stupidity unless you allow it to be.

E) I could be reading a book. Time is also a limited resource. You can respond to a comment on Facebook with an opinion no one will care about in a hundred years, or you can do something. Right now. You can take a walk by the river. Or you can kiss someone. Or you can jump on a trampoline.

I went to a trampoline place a few weeks ago. Little kids were running up to this slanted trampoline and doing flips. I wanted to do that. But I'm too old. Kids aren't afraid of doing a flip and breaking their necks and then being paralyzed for life. But as soon as I'm in the air, all I can imagine is my neck snapped off from the rest of my body. Would I pay anything to return to that age when I still wet the bed but could do a flip on the trampoline? No. Never. That would be a waste of my time. But I love myself anyway.

F) Loneliness. I think most people fight because they are alone. There's nothing we can do about loneliness in the material world. We've been trapped in these bodies since birth. But we try. We want people to agree with us so that for a brief second we can feel good about ourselves, establish a connection, and then make slow, sweet love.

Only the third part doesn't really happen. But we think it will. There are better ways to combat my loneliness than to hold onto an opinion that makes me the same as the other 49.9 percent of the world who share that opinion.

G) I'm always wrong. I have never had a correct opinion. I don't even know what a correct opinion smells like. When I first wrote in a prior book that zero wars can be justified, someone mentioned some Polynesian war from "Before Christ," or the Peloponnesian war. I don't know. Some war from two thousand years ago. I don't remember; I wasn't listening to his stupid opinion. See! That's what happens with opinions. Even I'm guilty of it.

Opinions are like money. No matter how much you know, there's always someone who knows more. And they aren't afraid to flaunt it. I have no credentials on anything. My education is hopelessly outdated. And my ten-year-old child constantly corrects me. The other day I tried to convince her that the United States was a republic and not a democracy. But she wouldn't change her opinion (see "A" above) even though I was telling her a FACT. When I give an opinion, I know that opinion works for me, right then. But that's about it. I don't always need to fight for the glory.

H) Hold your breath. Try holding your breath for just thirty seconds. That's all it takes. **Try it right now** while you are looking at this line. Now…on the twenty-ninth second, do any opinions matter?

I) Less. I'm trying to have fewer things in my life right now. This doesn't always mean fewer trinkets that shine on a shelf. It also might mean fewer things that upset me. Fewer people who bother me. Fewer regrets about things that are long dead and buried. Fewer anxieties about a future that may or may not exist. I find that if I dig deep and throw away one thing a day, then I wake up the next day a little more peaceful. I don't need to have so many opinions. The fight will continue with or without me.

J) Bewildered. I like to try this exercise: every time I have a judgment about something, I change the punctuation at the end of the judgment from an exclamation point to a question mark. "She should do this!" becomes, "She should do this?" Or "Obama should legalize crack!" becomes "Obama should legalize crack?" And, dare I say it, "Nobody should go to elementary school anymore because it's a brainwashing concentration camp posing as a glorified babysitting service!" becomes "Really?"

Just try it. It's fun. Walk around bewildered all day. It's much more peaceful.

"That guy shouldn't shove me!" becomes "That guy shouldn't shove me?" We live in a strange world. Every day, a labyrinth to explore. Clues to unfold. It's like you wake up in the dentist's chair and get thrown out into the street. The light is strange, your eyes are dilated (because of those eye drops the dentist keeps forcing on me when I'm unconscious), you're groggy, people are very, very busy walking around you, paying with the currency of unhappiness now in order to reach their glorious futures someday...maybe.

And you wonder, what happens if I just sit here? If I enjoy the sunlight hitting me? If I laugh at the dilated, fuzzy, people? If I cry myself to sleep in your arms, before you become angry again and you try to beat me and strangle me with an electric cord?

The point is, don't focus on those things in the material world that you cannot control or possibly ever change, when you can focus on inner health, on your inner world, on the things that matter.

How to Release the God Hormone

I disgust myself. When I was six, I used to make fun of one kid for being heavier than me. When I was seven, I made fun of a kid for being Chinese. He was the only Chinese kid in the neighborhood. I was a seven-year-old racist. He was so upset that the principal had to talk to me. The punishment: we had to ride with each other on the bus every day. He was more upset about this than I was.

When I was nine, I was caught shoplifting football cards, which put an end to a successful, yearlong crime spree that included stealing everything from candy to Charlie Brown books to *Mad* books to baseball cards. My parents were so angry that they cancelled my upcoming birthday party. Then they never let me have one again. I still don't have birthday parties. Because I stole a football card.

I did lots of things. Things much later. Ugh. I can hardly think of it. The things that I would do. I'm like a psychopath or sociopath when I really get down to it. Worst of all, I go to the bathroom. I've never seen a more disgusting thing than my own human body going to the bathroom. Ugh.

Google: I need to talk to you about this! You are making a car that drives without a driver. You are making glasses that wire my brain right into the Internet. Why the hell can't you make it so I don't have to shit? Like, can't I wear glasses that do photosynthesis from the sun and turn it into nutrition for my body? Nutrition with no waste. Why, for everything I eat, do I have to generate waste? This is almost proof that Satan exists.

And even worse, some of the waste gets stuck. If you're not yet my age (forty-four) you'll soon know what I'm talking about. It gets stuck forever. I've switched diets recently. No carbs. No processed sugars. Not even gluten-free stuff, which is all a scam. And, I have to say, the quality of what comes out of me has become much better. Nor do I feel as stuffed.

So, okay, glass half full. Right?

Let me tell you the real bad news, though it won't seem that way. Our alien ancestors who created us also created simple tools (call them "triggers," if you will) so we can reprogram our bodies to be happy. What does happy mean? It means various chemicals get manipulated throughout the body. Cortisol levels go down. Cortisol is the fight-or-flight hormone. So, like, when you are sitting at your desk staring at a computer screen and you are worried your boss is going to yell at you, your cortisol levels are going through the roof.

In other words, your body wants to do what it would've done twenty thousand years ago (a microsecond in our evolutionary history) and basically run away as fast as possible or physically destroy whatever is scaring you. Fight or flight. Note the "OR." There really isn't an in-between that says, "Don't move and simply stare at your computer screen while you are simmering in unrequited anger and frustration." That wasn't part of the evolutionary plan. That's probably what the Neanderthals did—and look at what happened to them. They're dead. Every last one of them.

So what do you do, in our modern day and age? You sit there, you stare at the computer screen, you maybe type some words, but then your brain is distracted. You can't think. Your cortisol is through the roof and nothing is working it off. That's really horrible. The cortisol needs to be worked off. Or else. You are royally *******. You can get cancer, heart disease, strokes, Alzheimer's, the whole works.

And if you are like me—if you are like most people—then chances are this is happening to you every day. Here's what happens. The vagus nerve stretches from your brain to your stomach and hits every organ along the way (almost). It gets inflamed when your cortisol levels are too high for too long. The vagus nerve basically causes every disease known to mankind. High stress inflames it, as does bad food, smoking, etc. You get the drift.

What Suppresses the Inflammation?

Oxytocin, another hormone that the body is more than happy to release. Oxytocin performs two very important functions that allow the human race to continue. Both of these functions have various, beneficial, side effects.

1) Oxytocin is released when you have an orgasm. For men, interestingly, it is only released when you have an orgasm with someone you love.
2) Oxytocin is released when a woman is in labor. It helps the cervix stretch so it's in less pain. Women, that is. For

men, when the female cervix starts to expand it's the beginning of about nine years of agony.

Basically, oxytocin is the hormone there at the critical moments of life creation. It's the "life hormone." It also helps reduce cortisol levels (you know that feeling of relaxation you get after sex) and inflammation of the vagus nerve. (I sort of like that word: *vagus*. It's both "vague" and "vaginal.")

So I'm not going to point to all the research. You can Google it with your glasses. But basically, there are various ways you can trick the body into releasing oxytocin. The benefits are simple: you feel better and you will live longer, and you will reduce stress and be happier.

GIVE MONEY AWAY. Turns out that showing compassion in a visceral way like giving money is linked to higher levels of oxytocin. My guess is that giving to charity is not the way to do it. I prefer my method of being a superhero.

HUGGING. Touching and hugging release oxytocin—with hugging being more powerful than touching, and hugging someone you love being more powerful than both. So a hug is better than a handshake. But almost as good as hugging is imagining yourself being hugged or cuddled by someone you love. Huh. It's really funny how the brain does that.

FACEBOOK. I like to browse my Facebook time line and occasionally "Like" a photograph posted by a random friend from thirty years ago. I would never in a million years call that friend and say, "That was a real cute photo of your baby that you posted." But liking the photo is my way of connecting with someone that I felt close to at some point in my life, even if it was only because her locker was next to mine in junior high school. Guess what? Turns out, using social media in this way releases oxytocin. You know you feel good when you do it. Do it more. In particular, Facebook "like" all of my blog posts. [The funny thing is, someone has actually done this scientific research and demonstrated it. Not the part about liking my blog posts but about Facebook in general. Although liking my blog posts will certainly release oxytocin. You can start now if you want.]

LAUGHTER. I will tell you my pre-date secret. In the brief period when I was single in between separation and remarriage, I had a technique before every date. I would watch either Michael Cera doing comedy or Louis CK doing stand-up. This would get me laughing, make my oxytocin hormones go on fire, and then I'd go right into the date, with all my sex hormones raging. That's a plus. I would be temporarily funnier, with a half-life of about two hours. I knew after four hours I would be boring again so the date would have to be over by then. (I do this before talks, too.)

WALKING. Note, I didn't say take a run. Running is great for increasing the metabolism but so is eating better. Otherwise, for me at least, running is really hard. I hate it. But I love to walk. Walk in the sun. The sun is a nutrient. And a half hour won't kill you, despite what global warming people say. Walking outside, as you might guess, is statistically correlated with higher levels of oxytocin. Well, you say, I can't walk. I have meetings all day. If you can, try to take a walking meeting. This helps you bond more with the person you are meeting with, and you might even have an adventure along the way (guess what—scientific research shows that having an adventure with someone also releases oxytocin. I guess because when you are chasing wolves with someone then you know you will feel safer with them afterward). The last time I had a walking meeting with a friend, a guy started yelling at me from a car and I challenged him (with a smile on my face) to a fight. My friend had to drag me away while the guy was parking his car and getting ready to kill me. It was fun. It was an adventure. I felt thrilled.

PHONE CALL. It's good to talk to a friend. I don't have a lot of friends. I have about three people on my call list. Maybe four if I stretch it. Maybe five. I don't know. Maybe fifty. I like a lot of people, but I'm too shy to call them. Maybe I should. And just chat for a few minutes. Like we all used to do when we were kids. "Hey, how are you doing? What's up?" This feels good. It's like a vocal hug with someone we like. Vocally hug people today.

BEING TRUSTED. This is hard. You can't force people to trust you. And trusting someone doesn't release oxytocin. But being trusted does. So live your life in such a way that more and more people will trust you. Guess what: you will be viewed in a more charismatic way if people trust you than if people don't trust you. Why not try this? How can you be more trusted? Oh my god, why so many questions today? My hands are already tired. I'm about 1,497 words already.

LISTENING TO MUSIC. Just lying down and listening to music releases oxytocin. That's why women in labor are encouraged to listen to soothing music. That's why people having sex listen to soothing music. I don't even really know what soothing music means. I keep thinking of the '90s R&B group PM Dawn. But I'm sure there are better examples (Spandau Ballet?).

FOOD. Here is my oxytocin-rich meal: eggs, mixed with bananas and pepper. Each ingredient is known to release high levels of oxytocin. So why not eat them all together: something sweet, something savory, something spicy, a fruit, and some protein; it's all good. Eat a big plate of that and nothing else. BAM! You are off for the day on an oxytocin spurt.

And finally:

BREATHING. Deep breathing hypnotizes your body into thinking everything is calm. And, guess what, it's not like you are being hunted down by wild giraffes right now. Things are calm, relatively speaking. When your body is calm, so is your mind, and oxytocin gets released. Ah, your body is saying when it breathes deep, everything is safe. So now I have time to be happy.

This is all good and bad news.

The good news is that there is a chemical in your brain that when released, makes you feel good for up to two weeks. And if a lot of it is released, you either feel like you are having an orgasm for two weeks or, I don't know, like your cervix is being expanded for two weeks. I have no idea on that one.

The bad news is exactly the same. A CHEMICAL will make you feel good for two weeks. In other words, our basic, human bodies are no better than Pavlovian dogs—triggered to salivate when the right stimuli hits our two hundred thousand-year-old evolutionary brains. We're no better than the dogs. No better than the jellyfish that crawled out of the bottom of the ocean and then formed tentacles, then arms, then brains.

Forget all self-help. It's all garbage. It's all about this one silly chemical. The news lately is all about the Higgs-Boson, the "god particle." Well, oxytocin is the "god hormone."

That said, I'll do all of the above. I need my body functioning. I need to get rid of mental waste and physical waste and emotional waste. Why not?

But at the end of the day, it's spiritual waste that I'm after. And how do you get that? How do you get to that peculiar desire of trying to have no desires? Because when you expect nothing, you have the immense satisfaction of getting everything you want.

How do you get there?

It's not oxytocin. I won't be fooled into believing it. But if it makes me shit out my mental and emotional waste better then sign me up. Being happy is a good start. But oxytocin is just the flower. And you can't see the flower without the light. The goal is to be the light.

The Seven Habits of Highly Effective Mediocre People

I'm pretty mediocre. I'm ashamed to admit it. I'm not even being sarcastic or self-deprecating. I've never done anything that stands out as, "Whoa! This guy made it into outer space!" Or…"This guy has a bestselling novel!" Or…"If only Google had thought of this!" I've had some successes and some (well-documented) failures, but I've never reached any of the goals I had initially set. I've always slipped off along the way, off the yellow brick road, into the wilderness.

I've started a bunch of companies. Sold some. Failed at most of them. I've invested in a bunch of startups. Sold some. Failed at some, and the jury is still sequestered on a few others. I've written some books, most of which I no longer like. I can tell you overall, though, that everything I have done has been distinguished by its mediocrity, its lack of a grand vision, and any success I've had can be just as much put in the luck basket as the effort basket.

That said, all people should be so lucky. We can't all be grand visionaries. We can't all be Picassos. We want to grow our business, make our art, sell it, make some money, raise a family, and try to be happy. My feeling, based on my own experience, is that aiming for grandiosity is the fastest route to failure. For every Mark Zuckerberg, there are a thousand Jack Zuckermans. Who is Jack Zuckerman? I have no idea. That's my point. If you are Jack Zuckerman and are reading this, I apologize. You aimed for the stars and missed. Your reentry into the atmosphere involved a broken heat shield and you burned to a crisp by the time you hit the ocean. Now we have no idea who you are.

If you want to get rich, sell your company, have time for your hobbies, raise a halfway decent family (with mediocre children, etc.), and on occasion enjoy the sunset with your wife, here are some of my highly effective recommendations.

PROCRASTINATION. In between the time I wrote the last sentence and the time I wrote this one, I played (and lost) a game of chess. My king and my queen got forked by a knight. But hey, that happens. Fork me once, shame on me, etc.

Procrastination is your body telling you that you need to back off a bit and think more about what you are doing. When you procrastinate as an entrepreneur, it could mean that you need a bit more time to think about what you are pitching a client. It could also mean you are doing work that is not your forte and that you are better off delegating. I find that many entrepreneurs are trying to do everything when it would be cheaper and more time-efficient to delegate, even if there are upfront monetary costs associated with that. In my first business, it was like a lightbulb went off in my head the first time

I delegated a programming job to someone. Why did I decide finally to delegate at that particular point? I had a hot date. Which was infinitely better than me sweating all night on some stupid programming bug (thank you, Chet, for solving that issue).

Try to figure out why you are procrastinating. Maybe you need to brainstorm more to improve an idea. Maybe the idea is no good as is. Maybe you need to delegate. Maybe you need to learn more. Maybe you don't enjoy what you are doing. Maybe you don't like the client whose project you were just working on. Maybe you need to take a break. There's only so many seconds in a row you can think about something before you need to take time off and rejuvenate the creative muscles. This is not for everyone. Great people can storm right through. Steve Jobs never needed to take a break. But I do.

Procrastination could also be a strong sign that you are a perfectionist. That you are filled with shame issues. This will block you from building and selling your business. Examine your procrastination from every side. It's your body trying to tell you something. Listen to it.

ZERO-TASKING. There's a common myth that great people can multitask efficiently. This might be true but I can't do it. I have statistical proof. I have a serious addiction. If you ever talk on the phone with me, there's almost a 100 percent chance that I am simultaneously playing chess online. The phone rings, and one hand reaches for the phone and the other hand reaches for the computer to initiate a one-minute game. Chess rankings are based on a statistically generated rating system. I can easily compare how well I do when I'm on the phone compared with when I'm not on the phone. There is a three-point standard deviation difference. Imagine if I were talking on the phone and driving. Or responding to e-mails. It's the same thing I'm assuming: phone calls cause a three-point standard deviation subtraction in intelligence. And that's the basic multitasking we all do at some point or other.

So great people can multitask. Wonderful. But since, by definition, most of us are not great (99 percent of us are not in the top 1 percent), it's much better to single-task. Just do one thing at a time. When you wash your hands, don't try to brush your teeth. Hear the sound of the water, feel the water on your hands, scrub every part. Be clean. Focus on what you are doing.

Often, the successful mediocre entrepreneur should strive for excellence in ZERO-tasking. Do nothing. We always feel like we have to be "doing something" or we (or, I should say "I") feel ashamed. Sometimes it's better to just be quiet, to not think of anything at all. A very successful, self-made business-man once told me, "Never underestimate the power of a long, protracted silence."

Out of silence comes the greatest creativity.

Not when we are rushing and panicking.

FAILURE. As far as I can tell, Larry Page has never failed. He went straight from graduate school to billions. Ditto for Mark Zuckerberg, Bill Gates, and a few others. But again, by defini-tion, most of us are pretty mediocre. We can strive for great-ness but we will never hit it. That means we will often fail. Not ALWAYS fail. But often.

My last sixteen out of seventeen business attempts were failures. Ultimately, life is a sentence of failures, punctuated only by the briefest of successes. So the mediocre entrepreneur learns two things from failure: First he learns directly how to overcome that particular failure. He's highly motivated to not repeat the same mistakes. Second, he learns how to deal with the psychology of failure. Mediocre entrepreneurs fail A LOT. So they get this incredible skill of getting really good at dealing with failure. This translates to monetary success.

The mediocre entrepreneur understands that persistence is not the self-help cliché "Keep going until you hit the finish line!" It's "Keep failing until you accidentally no longer fail." That's persistence.

NOT ORIGINAL. I've never come up with an original idea in my life. My first successful business was making web software, strategies, and websites for Fortune 500 companies. Not an original idea but at the time, in the '90s, people were paying exorbitant multiples for such businesses. My successful investments all involved situations where I made sure the CEOs and other investors were smarter than me. One hundred percent of my zeros as an angel investor were situations where I thought I was smart. I wasn't. I'm mediocre.

The best ideas are when you take two older ideas that have nothing to do with each other, make them have sex with each other, and then build a business around the bastard, ugly child that results. The child who was so ugly nobody else wanted to touch it. Look at Facebook: combine the Internet with stalking. Amazing!

And, by the way, it was about the fifth attempt at such a social network. Twitter: combine Internet with antiquated SMS protocols. Ugly! But it works. eBay: combine e-commerce with auctions. The song "I'll Be There." Combine Mariah Carey with Michael Jackson. If Justin Bieber sang John Lennon's "Imagine," it would be a huge hit. I might even listen to it.

POOR NETWORKING. I'm that guy: you know, the one at the party who doesn't talk to anyone and stands in the corner. I never go to tech meet-ups. I usually say no to very nice networking dinner invitations. I like to stay home and read. When I was running businesses, I was often too shy to talk to my employees. I would call my secretary from downstairs and ask if the hallway was clear then ask her to unlock my door and I'd hurry upstairs and lock the door behind me. That particular company failed disastrously.

But many people network too much. Entrepreneurship is hard enough. It's twenty hours a day of managing employees, customers, meetings, and product development. And the buck stops here sort of thing. And then what are you going to do? Network all night? Save that for the great entrepreneurs. Or the ones who are about to fail. The mediocre entrepreneur works his twenty hours, then relaxes when he can. It's tough to make money. Not a party.

DO ANYTHING TO GET A "YES." Here's a negotiation I did. I was starting stockpickr.com and meeting with the CEO of thestreet.com. He wanted his company to have a percentage of stockpickr.com, and in exchange he would fill up our ad inventory. I was excited to do the deal. I said, "Okay, I was thinking you would get 10 percent of the company." He laughed and said, "No. Fifty percent." He didn't even say, "We would like 50 percent." He just said, "Fifty percent." I then used all my negotiating skills and came up with a reply. "Okay. Deal."

I'm a salesman. I like people to say yes to me. I feel insecure when they say no or, even worse, if they don't like me. When I started a company doing websites, we were pitching to do Miramax.com. I quoted a price of $50,000. They said,

"No more than \$1,000, and that's a stretch." I used my usual technique: "Deal!"

But the end results: in one case, thestreet.com had a significant financial stake so that gave them more psychological stake. And for my first business, Miramax was now on my client list. That's why Con Edison had to pay a lot more. Often, the secret poor negotiator's keep is that we get more deals done. I get the occasional loss leader, and then ultimately the big fish gets reeled in if I get enough people to say yes. It's like asking every girl on the street to have sex with you. One out of a hundred will say yes. In my case it might be one out of a million but you get the idea.

POOR JUDGE OF PEOPLE. The mediocre entrepreneur doesn't "Blink" in the Malcolm Gladwell sense. In Gladwell's book, he often talks about people who can form snap, correct judgments in two or three seconds. My initial judgment when I meet or even see people is this: I hate you.

And then I veer from that to too trusting. Finally, after I bounce back and forth, and through much trial and error, I end up somewhere in the middle. I also tend to drop people I can't trust very quickly. I think the great entrepreneur can make snap judgments and be very successful with it. But that doesn't work for most people.

At this point, when I meet someone, I make sure I specifically don't trust my first instincts. I get to know people more. I get to understand what their motivations are. I try to sympathize with whatever their position is. I listen to them. I try not to argue or gossip about them before I know anything. I spend a lot more time getting to know the people whom I want to bring closer. I have to do this because I'm mediocre, and I'm a lot more at risk of bringing the wrong people into my circle.

So by the time I've decided to be close to someone—a client, an employee, an acquirer, an acquiree, a wife, etc.—I've already done a lot of the thinking about them. This means I can't waste time thinking about other things, like how to put a rocket ship on Jupiter. But overall it's worked.

"I thought being mediocre is supposed to be bad?" one might think. Shouldn't we strive for greatness? And the answer is, "Of course we should! But let's not forget that nine out of ten motorists think they are 'above average drivers.'" People overestimate themselves. Don't let overestimation get in the way of becoming fabulously rich, or at least successful enough that you can have your freedom, feed your family, and enjoy other things in life.

Being mediocre doesn't mean you won't change the world. It means being honest with yourself and the people around you. And being honest at every level is really the most effective habit of all if you want to have massive success.

How to Be Less Stupid

One has to balance mediocrity, though. With the human mind, it wants to take us below mediocrity. If given the chance, the human mind will constantly fill us up with thoughts. You would think thoughts make us smart, but it's quite the opposite.

I'm really stupid. I can tell you in advance. I think at heart, if I work at it, I can be smart. But at the moment, I'm largely an idiot. I feel that I have the right knowledge but I let a lot of stuff get in the way. My head fills up too quickly with thoughts.

You know, "stuff": worries, guilt, paranoia, grudges, and resentment. Like, for instance, I resent the people who resent me. I think they resent me for no reason. So now I resent them. What a circle-jerk!

I used to think that when I added stuff to my brain I'd get smarter. But this is not true. For instance, if I look up when Charlemagne was born I'd just add a fact to my head that I will forget tomorrow but will clutter my subconscious mind. This won't make me smarter.

Subtraction, and not addition, is what makes the window to the brain more clear, wipes away the smudges, and opens the drapes.

In the '90s I had an important business meeting. I was trying to convince Tupac's manager to let me do his website and enhanced CD (this was right after he died). Not only was the meeting bad, but it was embarrassing.

The manager asked me to put my demo CD into the computer and show him what I had. The only problem: his computer was running Windows. At that point I had never in my life used a Windows machine, only Macs and Unix. So I had no idea how to put the CD in there and get it running. He laughed me out of the room.

I had a chess lesson afterwards. I couldn't play at all. It was like I didn't even know the rules. My instructor, a chess grandmaster, said, "What's wrong with you today?" I was ashamed. And angry at myself. So my intelligence went way down—like 80 percent down.

So many things have put useless, wasteful, thoughts in my head. If you think back to all of your best moments in life, were they moments when there were tons of thoughts happening in your head? Or moments when there were fewer thoughts, i.e., when you were calm and contemplative?

If I want to be happy and productive, I think back to those moments of pain and try to figure out what was going on in my head that made me so miserable that I couldn't function.

Paranoia is certainly one of them. Waking up in the middle of the night and wondering: is she cheating? Is he stealing? Are they talking about me? Will they sue me? Etc. You lose about 30 to 50 percent of your intelligence. That's a big chunk. For me, it's because I can't think of anything else. I would circle her house until the lights were on and then I'd knock on the door. Or I would go to his office and not leave until he showed up. Paranoia will destroy you.

Sometimes, in the middle of the day, I'll also experience an extreme attack of resentment. What for? Over someone who wrote about me a year ago? Or someone who blocked an opportunity for me for reasons only he knows. Who knows why people do these things? They are just as unconscious as everyone else. Our goal is to be conscious. To be the one who is aware of the actions and reactions around us. We have to be, if we're going to be a Choose-Yourself-er. Otherwise we will get stuck in the same no-passing lane everyone else is slowly driving in.

I figure I lose at least 20 percent of my intelligence when I am resentful. Maybe 30 percent if I throw feelings of revenge on top of it. Does it really help me to think of which particular bat I will use to take out my revenge fantasy?

Regret is another one it took me years to deal with in my worst moments. I've written about it a billion times. I lost a lot of money in 2000–2001. I regret it. Or, I should say, I regretted it. I don't anymore. How come? Because I saw that regret was taking at least 60 percent of my intelligence away. I couldn't afford 60 percent. I could afford 2 percent, not 60 percent. I didn't start coming up with ideas for new businesses until the regret went away.

Brene Brown has written an excellent book called *The Gift of Imperfection*, but I'll summarize it here: perfectionism is sometimes the most dangerous set of thoughts you can let make their home in your head. When I was running a fund, I never wanted to have a down month. I'd be afraid to talk to my investors. One guy, who is still a good friend (I spoke with him today even) said, "Listen, if you're going to be a fund manager you have to be able to talk to people when you have a down month."

But I was ashamed. When I lost my house, I moved seventy miles away. I didn't want to run into anyone. I felt shame. When I write a blog post I think is weak, I might take it down before too many see it. I'm ashamed of it. I want to win the Nobel Prize for blog writing. Or get at least ten thousand Facebook "like"s. But I can't control that; I'm imperfect. The shame of imperfectionism takes at least 20 percent of my intelligence away. Because people sense and appreciate honesty, and honesty about imperfections, believe it or not, creates enormous opportunities. I've seen it happen in my own life.

And related to perfectionism is certainly the feeling that you want to control the events around you. I want to control everything around me. But sometimes things are bad and there's nothing you can do about it. Sometimes you have to surrender and say, "This is bad now but good things will happen later." Then a great weight lifts off your shoulders.

You know why they always say a great weight lifts off your shoulders? Because that's where your brain is. And your brain is heavy. It rests on your shoulders. When stuff is weighing it down you lose about 10 to 20 percent of your intelligence. Give up control and get smarter. A simple example: you are late for a meeting but there's traffic. You can think, God damn this traffic. Why am I always in traffic? Or you can be thinking about something smart: like how good bacon tastes. Can I make a better bacon? Or how would I start a helicopter airline to take me from one side of the city to the other. These seem like dumb thoughts. But they are much better than "God damn this traffic!"

Even worse than trying to control the future is feeling a total lack of control over things that have already happened in the past. This is regret. A good friend of mine wrote me recently. I should say, wrote me six weeks ago. Every day when I wake up I tell myself: don't return e-mails until you read, then write. But then sometimes I have other things to do. Meetings. Or BS stuff. Or eating. I say, "Okay, I will return that e-mail later." And then when later comes, I feel bad that I hadn't returned his e-mail earlier. Then, at 3 a.m., I'll turn over and say to Claudia, "I didn't return that e-mail". She'll say, "Urgh...ushghsh...emmmm," which was not the answer I was looking for. Then I don't sleep as much. Then I feel guilty. That takes away about 10 percent of my intelligence right there.

First there's the past but then there's the distant future. We ultimately have no way to predict the future. But our mind does one thing over and over that leaves us less intelligent: it constantly puts us in a fantasy world that includes our worst-case scenario. Let's say I lose $1,000 in the stock market one day. Sometimes I think to myself, "Holy shit, if I lose that amount every day for the next..." And it gets worse and worse. My worst-case scenarios have my children begging for food on the harsh streets of Bangalore. I've spent at least a year of my life, when you add it up, thinking of the worst-case scenario. Even though the worst-case scenario HAS NEVER HAPPENED. Or if it does happen, it was never as bad as I thought it would be. I have a scarcity complex. If I didn't have that then I'd have an "abundance complex." And I firmly believe abundance follows an abundance complex. So I'm smarter (and wealthier) when I give up that scarcity complex.

If we truly want to learn, we never learn when we are talking. We only learn when we are listening. Claudia wanted to say something important to me. But I spoke instead. I imparted my great wisdom on her before she could get a word out. Finally, she forgot what she was going to say. Probably because my words were so wise they were like the Bible. Or like *Robert's Rules of Order*. Or *Strunk & White*. That's how wise I am. *STRUNK & WHITE!* Extra talking probably takes away at least 15 percent of my intelligence. Because I could've been listening and learning. Or reading about grammar. Or not getting into an accident when talking on the phone. Sometimes we just have to Shut Up!

I was talking to a friend of mine the other day. She was giving me every reason why she couldn't succeed. Her age. Her looks. Her privacy ("I can never write what I want"), her lack of time, and so on. Everyone has excuses. Everyone says "I can't." I can't be a medical professional unless I go to medical school. I can't be a filmmaker unless I raise $10 million to make a movie. I can't marry a supermodel because I'm ugly. I can't I can't I can't. For every "can't," you should send me $10. I can do all those things. Particularly if I have your $10.

Don't hit yourself over the head when these thoughts are in your brain. Just notice when these things come up. It's not like you're going to get cured of paranoia. But notice when it appears. Water withers the rock away. Every time you notice, the window clears a tiny bit. A smudge is gone. You get a glimpse of the light outside.

You get a tiny bit smarter. Maybe later you have to look for the deeper emotional reasons for why you feel the way you do. And there are a lot of reasons. Everyone could've made fun of your acne in junior high school and now you want to be loved by everyone. (Err, maybe that happened to me.) But right now, this second, just don't get hit by a car when you cross the street.

You can say, "Hey, wait a second! All of those things equal up to more than 100 percent!" Well, what can I say? You're smarter than me.

Honesty Makes You More Money

Admit it: you were jealous of Bernie Madoff. For a split second. That night in December 2008, when you first heard the news, interrupting the ongoing panic of every bank going out of business, every job disappearing, every ATM machine running out of cash, the organic fruit at the farmers market skyrocketing to $200 an apple. For a brief moment, you heard that news and you thought, "He stole $65 billion. Man, I would've had cosmetic surgery on my face and then moved to Brazil with that kind of money."

Then the truth came out. The news that the money was never there in the first place. The suicides. The owner of the Mets managed to get his money back just in time.

A woman from Minnesota called me, crying, saying, "Why is it they keep going on about the poor Jews who lost their money. I'm a Christian and I lost my last $800,000." Every day, as more news came out, the entire horror story kept getting more real.

Madoff in jail. His wife left with a measly million or two and finally the horror of their son killing himself.

But, for a moment, there was: What would I do with $65 billion?

And then, the false reality that went through everyone's head: the only way to make a lot of money in this world is to lie and steal.

I get that question a lot in my Twitter Q&A sessions: Why is it that you have to be dishonest to succeed in this world? And people don't believe me when I say that's not true. In fact, the exact opposite is true. Only honesty will succeed. They say back, "That has not been my experience."

Nobody asks: Do you have to be dishonest to succeed? People seem to know the answer already, and they want to know, structurally, why is this truth?

Capitalism is still suffering from the mortal blow that was struck in 2008. Everyone was a crook. And Madoff was just the tip of the iceberg. Mubarak's family ran away with $200 billion by the time he was kicked out of Egypt. Every day I get news in my inbox of another Ponzi scheme. Yesterday it was a $4.9 million hedge fund down in some backwater swamp county in Florida.

"Why?" people want to know. People want some justification. Maybe they are really asking, "Okay, I've been avoiding it until now but should I take the plunge and start being dishonest in order to make money?" And then maybe the next question, "Can you give a 'top ten' for how to be dishonest and make money?"

The problem is this: they are completely wrong. Dishonesty never works. **Honesty is the only way to make money in today's world.**

Nobody believes me on this. People laugh at me. "Don't you know anything? Of course dishonest people step on the honest people and have more success." People want to justify their own failures and use their pretend-goodness to explain why they didn't start Google, or steal $65 billion, or get that last promotion when the backstabbing bitch from aisle 3 got the raise after doing who knows what.

But here's the truth.

Dishonesty works…until it doesn't. Everyone messes up. And when you are dishonest, you are given only one chance and then it's over. You're out of the game—at least until you get your act straight and you have to start from scratch with your tail between your legs.

HONESTY COMPOUNDS. It compounds exponentially. No matter what happens in your bank account, in your career, in your promotions, in your startups. Honesty compounds exponentially, not over days or weeks, but years and decades. More people trust your word and spread the news that you are a person to be sought out, sought after, given opportunity, given help, or given money. This is what will build your empire.

I know this through countless failures. The more times I fail but communicate about it, the more times I make no money at all but let someone have ideas for free; the more times I try to "get mine" but only end up getting stabbed by those who think it's okay to be dishonest, the greater the number of seeds I've planted and the more money I'll make in the long run.

Be dishonest once, and all of those seeds will be washed away in a thunderstorm of life-killing proportions. A hurricane of despair that will sweep away all of your opportunities forever.

You are left with a desert and will have to start again.

How You Can Be More Honest In Your Life:

GIVE CREDIT. Even if the ideas were all yours. Even if you made nothing on them. Even if they were blatantly stolen. Give credit and move on. Hoarding your ideas for the moment when you can shine, will only leave you by yourself in a dimly lit room with only a mirror to stare at.

BE THE SOURCE. "But if I give ideas for free, what if they could've made a billion dollars? I always get screwed by my partners." If you are the source of ideas, then you are ALWAYS the source. Forget the losers who steal. Move on. You become THE fountain of ideas. People come to the fountain and make wishes and throw money in. Don't be a trickle of dirty water. Be the fountain and let people know it by giving away all credit and rewards.

A great example of "the source" is Google. Google has absolutely no content on it. There's nothing there but a little box. You go to that magic box and you enter in a term you want to know about. Let's say, "motorcycles."

Then Google is completely honest. They come back right away and say, "We know ABSOLUTELY NOTHING about motorcycles BUT if you go to these ten or so websites, we think these are the best sites where you can find out about motorcycles."

"Oh! And by the way," Google continues, "here's three more sites that know about motorcycles, but we are being totally honest here, those three sites are paying us. Just so you know."

And then you leave Google. The average person spends only a few minutes A MONTH at Google. In fact, the longer you stay at Google, the less profitable Google is. They want you to get the hell off their site. Every time you leave their site, either their algorithm improves (they learn from what you click on), or they make money (you click on a site that paid them).

And then where do you go when you want to find out about, say, contraceptives? You go to Google. You go to the source.

When I first started in the Internet business, I was advising big companies on how to create a web presence. The one thing nobody wanted to do was to link out to other websites. This was the exact opposite of what has now become the Choose Yourself era.

The Choose Yourself era means you have the confidence to be honest. The confidence to go up against the big corporations that refuse to choose you. The confidence to direct traffic to those people who might have more resources than you have.

To choose yourself you must first be fearless. To know that abundance is everywhere, not just hidden behind the masks you wear to display your skills to the public.

INTRODUCE TWO PEOPLE. Every day you can think of at least two people to introduce to each other who will help each other. You don't have to be in the middle. "Take me off cc," you should say. Let them help each other. Let them benefit. You don't need to be in the middle and benefit this time. You'll benefit next time. Or the time after that. Even if it means giving up opportunities for yourself if you think someone else would be better for the job.

Think of it this way: There's the "linear effect" and there's the "network effect." If you live life linearly, your value and resources only go up every time you meet someone new and the list of people *you* know becomes bigger. This is not good enough anymore. You must create your own empire. And you can't do it one at a time. That's not an empire, that's a list.

The network effect, on the other hand, has been well known on the Internet since its early days. The premise is that the value of a site goes up exponentially depending on how many people are using it. The more people using the site who don't know each other or didn't learn about the site from each other, the stronger the network effect. It's the Empire Builder.

How does this apply to you? How many people are "using you?" The value of your network goes up exponentially when you view your contacts and resources not as a list but as a network of nodes on a graph. Think of the number of connections that can connect two different nodes on that graph. It's exponential compared to the number of items in a list that connect directly to you.

The way you create the network effect is by encouraging people in your network to connect to each other and to help each other.

It feels funny sometimes. Sometimes people say to me, "Oh, I met so-and-so, thanks to your blog." And I think to myself, "HEY! THAT'S MY SO-AND-SO!" I have to stop that feeling. It's only limiting. The universe has limitless resources. You have limited resources and limited time. The only way to create abundance is to behave more like the universe.

Set the conditions for life. Then sit back and watch the matings occur. Before long you will have created life, you will have helped create the many great things that your connections will create together. Once again you have become the source.

TAKE THE BLAME. I messed up in October 2008. I was going through a separation and financial crisis, and I was scared out of my mind. I was managing a little bit of money a hedge fund had allocated me. I was down that month. It was ground zero of the goddamn financial crisis. I would sleep in my hammock until it would rain and storm all over me and the next thing I would know the Dow was down another seven hundred points while I was soaked and sick and angry. The hedge fund manager called me at the end of the month and said, "Look, I've called you ten times and you didn't return the call. Just return the call once and it would've been okay. Now I've got to take the money back." He was right. And I told him that. Eventually. We're good friends now and have worked together since but it took a few years to build back the trust.

"A 'No' uttered from the deepest conviction is better than a 'Yes' merely uttered to please, or worse, to avoid trouble."
— Gandhi

DON'T LEAD A DOUBLE LIFE. Everything you do takes up space in your brain. If you live a double life (and you know what I mean if I'm talking to you), then that extra life takes up neurons and synapses working overtime. The brain can't handle it. It starts to degrade instead of grow. Living a double life might've given you momentary pleasure but now your brain is heading straight for the gutter. And your finances, which are a reflection of the health of your brain, will fall straight into the sewer with it.

DON'T BE ANGRY. Anger is a form of dishonesty. Nobody is perfect. It's a lie to expect the people around you to be perfect. Sometimes I'm angry with my kids. But they are just kids. Sometimes I'm angry at people I'm trying to do deals with. But they have their own motivations, fears, worries, and anxieties. They don't have to do everything I expect of them. So my anger is really a belief that they should do what I expect them to do. It's a form of dishonesty when you lie to yourself about the expectations you have of others. Of course, you can't control your anger. Sometimes it just happens. But note it for what it is, examine it, and try to turn it around, even just a little—in order to learn more about yourself rather than to blame someone else. That's where the honesty will compound.

NO EXCUSES. When I lost money in October 2008, it was easy to blame a manipulated market and all the criminals who led it to be that way. When I lost millions of dollars in 2000 to the point of going completely broke and losing my home, it was easy to blame an "Internet bust" and "corrupt CEOs" rather than my own lack of experience in the financial world. Excuses are easy lies we tell ourselves to cover up our failures. One such excuse is, only dishonest people get ahead. This is also a lie.

MAKE OTHERS LOOK GOOD. This is more than just giving credit. There's a commonly quoted rule in management, the "Pareto Rule," which states that 80 percent of the work is done by 20 percent of the people. This is, in part, a product of an inferior standardized educational system where kids for twenty years are encouraged to do the minimum required to pass and make it to the next "level" on some imaginary ladder of success. But everyone wants to be acknowledged for small achievement. Take out your microscope. Acknowledge even the smallest accomplishments of the people around you. Bring more and more of the people around you into the 20 percent. At heart, everyone wants to be perceived as special. That's because everyone *is* special but are often never acknowledged that way. Be different. Be aware of the smallest movements around you and acknowledge them. Nobody will forget that.

DON'T GOSSIP. One time I trashed an entrepreneur I had invested in to another investor. Later that day I was supposed to have dinner with the first entrepreneur. By that time, just four hours later, he had heard I trashed him. He never trusted me again. People always hear. And if they don't hear, they feel, because word gets around. And you can't predict this. And it's another way of living a double life.

DO WHAT YOU SAY YOU ARE GOING TO DO. Be that guy.

ENHANCE THE LIVES OF OTHERS. In 1999 some of my employees in my first company left and started a competitor company. Some of my partners were mad. I encouraged the employees. How come? Because nobody needs to be my employee for their entire lives. Always help people grow into their own potential. The only thing I tell these people is, "If you ever find me in the gutter with a needle sticking out of my elbow, please help me out." They laugh and say, "That will never happen." Believe me. Anything can happen. I've been helped out of that gutter more than once.

Ten years later I ran into the employee who became CEO of that spinoff company. He ran after me and called my name. It was in Times Square in New York. We hadn't spoken in almost ten years. His company had greatly expanded. They had taken in major investors, and the company was now profitable and had lots of employees. He told me that when he walked the floor, he always pictured two people as his role models: his commander in the Israeli Army. And me. I felt really honored. He had greatly helped me when I was building my business. And now it was an honor for me to help him back in that way. I don't ever have to benefit off of his business. But his business is helping many people now and, in its own way, that creates abundance for me. The abundance can never stop when you help others.

I haven't always been honest. I try. And I hope I'm getting better. I try every day to improve and to follow the advice I've just given you. Otherwise I wouldn't have given it. But I've seen it. With people who have been in business for ten, twenty, forty years. Honesty compounds little by little. And that compounding turns into millions or billions. The dishonest people disappear. They die. They go to jail. They don't maximize their potential. They run. They are scared.

You will have nobody to run from. Some people will hate you. Some people will doubt your sincerity. But the people who need someone to call, someone to share with, or someone to give to, these people will know who to call. They will call you.

You're Never Too Young to Choose Yourself: Nine Lessons from Alex Day

I wish I had been smarter when I was twenty-three years old. I did everything wrong: I felt like I needed a college degree. I felt like I needed a graduate degree (I was ultimately thrown out of graduate school). I felt like I needed a publishing company to "choose me" to be a writer. I felt like I needed a big corporation to hire me so I could validate that I was smart, that it was okay for me to be successful.

I needed none of these things.

You need none of these things.

The world has changed, become different. The middleman is on life support, the barriers to entry have come down, and the Choose Yourself era has fully arrived.

Alex Day is a perfect example. If you've never heard of Alex Day, that's okay. Most people haven't. But enough have. And they LOVE him. Alex is a twenty-three-year-old musician from

England. Since 2009, when he was nineteen, he's released three studio albums, had three UK Top40 hits, and accrued 100-plus million views on his YouTube channel. He did *all of it* with no record label and mostly just the support of his YouTube fans. His third, most recent album came out in the UK the same day as Justin Timberlake's long-awaited, much-discussed *20/20 Experience* album (his third, also).

Here's the result:

TOP ALBUMS >

1. **What About Us - EP**
   The Saturdays

2. **Bad Blood**
   Bastille

3. **Unorthodox Jukebox**
   Bruno Mars

4. **Fade (feat. Maiday) - EP**
   Jakwob

5. **The Next Day (Deluxe Version)**
   David Bowie

6. **The High Hopes EP**
   Kodaline

7. **Our Version of Events (Special E...**
   Emeli Sandé

8. **Epigrams and Interludes**
   Alex Day

9. **The 20/20 Experience (Deluxe V...**
   Justin Timberlake

10. **The Truth About Love**
    P!nk

Snapshot of the itunes chart the day after both albums were released

Justin Timberlake is like the crown prince of the music industry. The labels love him. The radios love him. He tours everywhere. He has a massive marketing machine behind him. And he's married to Jessica Biel. That's all pretty good.

But not enough. Alex Day beat him. How the hell did that happen? I had no idea. So I called up Alex and asked him.

Lesson Number One about Choosing Yourself: I can choose myself to call anyone I want. If they want to talk to me, great.

Here is my interview with Alex, re-printed in its entirety (it's got too much good stuff just to excerpt):

Me: I read you started posting videos on YouTube in 2006. How long before you felt, "This is it. This is going to be something big."

Alex: Right from my first thirty subscribers, I began talking to the audience that was there and making videos directly for them and replying to comments, but I never saw it as a "fan base"—I mainly just figured we were all bored kids. My first experience of being treated like a celebrity of sorts was not until four years later in 2010, when I did a few gigs with a band I was in at the time (comprised of YouTubers) and would go to really small parts of the UK like Norwich and there'd be two hundred people there all screaming for us and going crazy.

Me: Ultimately, you need money though, to be an artist. You can't be a starving artist forever. When you don't go with a big label you have three choices: YouTube ads, iTunes downloads, and performing. Which of these avenues worked for you?

Alex: Performing wasn't an avenue for me—the only gigs I've done are one-off launch events (to launch my album for example) or gigs with friends (as I mentioned). I really don't feel the need to gig when I can reach my audience online and hit everyone at once, all over the world, and not exclude anybody, which a tour doesn't do.

Lesson Number Two: All the conventional methods for making money and distribution are out the window because the barriers to entry that create the premium value are gone.

Alex: Of the other two—I released my first musical thing (a compilation of YouTube covers called YouTube Tour) in 2007, I think it was, and it made a couple hundred bucks. Then in 2008 they introduced the YouTube partnership program and I was one of the first partners. Back then I made maybe $300 a month. Then it slowly rose, and at the same time my first album came out in October 2009, so with the money from that plus YouTube I moved out in March 2010 to a place with my best friend and we paid £600 each on rent so it wasn't too bad. It used to be about equal what I made from YouTube and what I made from music, but since "Forever Yours" got to #4 in 2011, my music sales have been way more than my YouTube. Typically I make around £3500 a month from YouTube (I'm on a network so they can sell the ad space higher) and at least £10,000 a month from music and merch sales. I've also done other projects—I co-created a card game with my cousin, which we sell online. I have a business called Lifescouts that I launched this year—which add a bit of extra cash to the pot also.

Me: Isn't this a little like what Ani DiFranco did? She never signed with a major label. She just did her own thing.

Alex: I think the main difference was she was constantly touring and I never have. Also she got her independence by forming her own label. I don't have a label at all.

Me: Have the labels ever reached out to you?

Alex: Labels have never known what the hell to do with me. I always went in with an open mind—I don't like the idea that being proudly unsigned/independent instantly means I'm white and they're black and we have to duel to the death or whatever. There are a lot of things I do on my own because I have to, so I've got good at them, but it would definitely be easier with outside help! So I was willing to hear what they could offer and how we could work together and I still would be, but I don't think labels are ready to be that humble. They want to control everything. I like being able to decide my own songs and film my own music videos. I've had several meetings with Island Records in the UK, the last of which ended with the guy saying he doesn't think I'm ready to be on a label yet because "We only signs artists we can sell at least a million copies of in the next three months"—but if he's waiting for me to get to that point without him, why do I need the label ever? I've also met with Warner, Sony, EMI—they were all the same. None of them expected to justify themselves, and at best they were just trying to "figure out my secret," and at worst they were completely uninformed and lazy (see my video on the subject, which sums it up better than I ever could here.).

Me: But what would you use the labels for now?

Alex: I guess it would be great to get their help. I'll give you an example. I write my music, play my music, make my videos, design the albums, and so on, but it does provide some validation to be in physical stores.

So a ten-year-old kid who liked my stuff told his dad he should work with me. The dad was with distribution with Universal. So I did a one-off distribution deal with Universal where I did everything but they got me in every HMV. It was great. Nobody said I could sell physical CD singles but I sold ten thousand in the UK.

Lesson Number Three: Everyone will say you CAN'T. Especially when you're young, but if you pick and choose how to work with the entrenched system, you CAN.

Lesson Number Four: The power of the community you build will be felt in ways you can't predict (a ten-year-old fan, for instance).

Me: You clearly have a long-run view of what artists should be doing and where the industry is going. Where do you think the music industry will be in ten years?

Alex: I don't think it matters where I see the music industry in ten years—I look at where the music industry is now and it's not helping me, so I've learned to exist without it! What I'd like in ten years is for the music industry to be in a place where it supports me more, but that's a long time to hope for that. The thing with the long-run view is that it's actually a series of short spurts. It's more like the general public are on the second floor of a building and every single/music video I release affords me a bounce on a trampoline outside. So for a second I'm up to the window saying, "Heyguyslookatme," and then if they don't see me I just fall down again and make a new song and try again. If one of my tracks catches fire, it'll all happen very quickly, but when it doesn't you just have to try again.

Lesson Number Five: Persistence is more important than industry validation because it's not the industry that is buying what you're selling.

Lesson Number Six: Focus on what you can do for your art/ business right now instead of trying to aim for things ten years for now.

Me: What should most artists/creators do to keep going when things look their most frustrating? Most people give up. And, frankly, most people are no good. How did you keep going from 2006 to now, even when things looked bleak?

Alex: To help with knowing if you're good or not, **you need a mentor. (Lesson Number Seven)** You have to have someone who either knows the industry or knows what's commercial or successfully experimental or whatever it is you're trying to achieve with your music and can tell you honestly whether or not you're meeting that standard. I have a now-very close friend who used to work in the industry a lot, broke songs like "Who Let the Dogs Out" and "I Get Knocked Down But I Get Up Again"—we met through a mutual friend and I would just send him songs and he would say "not a hit, not a hit, not a hit" until eventually I sent him "Forever Yours" and he said "You've done it! Now break it."

He didn't help me, he just advised, but you need someone like that who you trust. The other thing with giving up is that I simply can't. Sometimes I have low points and I spend a month or two not working on music at all, but then someone will play me an amazing new song, or I'll watch one of my music videos back, or watch the Grammy's and I think "I have to be doing this." I can't give up because I want it too much, and however hard it might be, it'll be worse if I wasn't pursuing what I love.

Lesson Number Five (redux): Persistence, there it is again.

Me: How did you get into all of this? How did you build the so-called ten thousand hours to be an expert?

Alex: I grew up with my mum listening to the radio whenever we were around the house, driving to and from school, etc. Music's always been a huge part of my life. And there's so much more to learning about good songwriting than the actual writing, in the same way writers tell you to read a lot if you want to be a good writer. My favorite part about developing as an artist is spending hours listening to music, listening to every Michael Jackson song and looking for commonalities, patterns, the way the production sounds, how the style varies. I've been known to draw out graphs that plot the melody of a chorus so then I can see visually how a song moves and how it varies from track to track. I started writing songs when I was thirteen. I started writing not-bad songs when I was seventeen. I wrote "Forever Yours" when I was twenty-two and the rest of the songs on my new collection last year at age twenty-three so I've been doing it ten years now and I know I still have a lot to learn. In a way that's the most exciting thing—to hear the difference in the songs I'm making between this year and the last, and then think "What will I be making by NEXT year?"—there's always room to grow and that's exciting.

Me: How do you engage your fans outside of your music? How do you "build the tribe," in Seth Godin speak?

Alex: It's just YouTube. I have Twitter and Facebook only because I sort of feel I have to, because I need to reach people in those places. That's not to say I'm just on auto-pilot on those places, but I'd much rather not have to use those services. Part of why it's necessary right now is that I don't have enough reach in the "real world" for me to allow other people to promote what I'm doing on my behalf, but my Twitter and Facebook are effectively work accounts that just update people on what I'm up to. For the personal connection, it's all YouTube. I love it there. It's such a creative outlet, I've been making videos for seven years and never got bored of it, one or two videos a week regularly all that time.

It genuinely saddens me when YouTube isn't lumped in as one of the essential social metrics with Twitter, Facebook and Tumblr (I do have a Tumblr, too, but like the others I don't really know how to use it)—I understand YouTube and it's changed my whole life. The main thing is that I don't always talk about music; in fact, I try to keep a 3:1 ratio of music videos to non-music videos. Other YouTube musicians spend all their time just doing covers or videos from tour, but it means what you can enjoy about that channel is reduced to whether or not you like that person's music. I just released a new music video and loads of the comments say "I never got into your sound/liked your music before but I really love this song" and those are long-term subscribers of mine—they've stayed because I can offer them other stuff, but it also means they'll give each new song a listen and sometimes they like it.

Lesson Number Eight: Pick your social media outlet, master it. It's not enough to master your art form. You have to personally master how you will distribute through some social medium, engage with fans, etc.

I admit I'm jealous of Alex. And I'm a big fan.

Lesson Number Nine, which is really hard for me: Talk to your big fans.

Congrats to Alex for continually choosing himself as far back as 2006, when he was seventeen, and not being shy about explaining the specifics, even the money, of how he did it. Alex is exceptional and, for now, the exception to the rule. But not for long. He can't be. Because eventually everyone will have to follow a similar path in the new economy we live in. Alex proves you're never too young to take the first step on that path.

THE CURIOUS CASE OF THE SEXY IMAGE

In a blog post I wrote once, I used the above image of a woman on a beach when I posted the link on Facebook. Someone accused me of always using images of half-naked women to promote a post.

He was correct. But I also pointed out that the picture was of a human being at the height of physical achievement. A state I will never be in, nor will any of the "half-naked" critics. And, by the way, technically she's only about *90 percent* naked. So there.

What's funny is that even in the comments to THAT post, someone asked, "Why do you always post pictures of half-naked women?"

First off, when is it so unusual to post pictures of half-naked women? Most men AND women's magazines do it. It's clearly an image that human beings like to look at.

Second, didn't you read the posts you just commented on?

And finally, the woman in the picture actually wrote me herself with a response to my critics.

Her name is Dashama. You can find her at www.dashama .com, where she offers courses on yoga. I strongly encourage anyone who thinks they can do the position in that picture—it's called Kapotasana, or "King Pigeon Pose"—to take her courses and try to better himself.

At first I guess I was relieved that she wasn't suing me for using her image without her permission. But after I read her message, it was interesting to see that Dashama, just like many of the people discussed in this book, came at the issue not from the external barriers that society imposes, but from the foundation of internal health she had built up that not only cured her physical disorders but helped her create a business and life most of us can only dream about.

Dashama wrote:

> *Dear James,*
> *A friend of mine forwarded me the link to your article featuring my yoga photo recently. I read the entire article*

and also about 8 others you have posted on various topics. I find your writing style both easy to read and conversational, with just enough humor and authenticity to keep the reader with you until the end. So in short, you're a great writer :)

The controversy around nakedness is always an interesting topic and I thought about the response you got to my photo for a while.

For the past 10 years I have been strengthening my 'It doesn't affect me when people pass judgment' muscles, since I know that what I do is from an authentic space of love and devotion to make a positive difference in the world. I came from a childhood of foster homes and poor health, so just to be alive now is a miracle every single day. The fact that I can put my leg behind my head and balance on my hands is even more miraculous than you may imagine, given that 10 years ago I was in a terrible car accident that cost me the curve in my cervical spine. After every doctor I saw told me there was nothing I could do to reverse that, I sought alternative options. Now, after almost a decade of self-sought healing, I am able to do some very miraculous things with my body that most people, as you commented, may only dream about.

Besides the physical miracle of my personal healing experience, the fact that I can be living my dreams and doing what I love as a career is even more inspiring to me. There was a time when I was the one sitting in a cubicle working an office job and hating my life. Judging myself and everyone around me and focusing on the negative. It took a tremendous leap of faith to decide what I loved to do and move toward making a career out of it. Then it took another 5 years of personal development inner work to get to the point that I could get past my limiting belief systems that held me back from my power and authentic self-expression. The rest of it was a steep learning curve of how to operate a business as a single woman in a male-dominated world; navigating these waters has not been an easy task.

Despite all of the challenges, it was the best decision of my life. The ROI has been paid to me with dividends of joy and not money, but I'll take that to the bank and cash it any day over doing something that kills my spirit just to pay the bills.

And that is what inspires me even more. That I know, in my heart and soul, that EVERYTHING IS POSSIBLE.

We rob ourselves of our joy and happiness when we stop and check in with what everyone else is thinking and saying about us.

This is a tragic recurrence that has to stop.

Years ago I read an interview with Gabrielle Reese where she was asked how she deals with the pressures of being a pro athlete, SI model, mother and wife of Surf God Laird Hamilton. She said, "In life, you will always have 30 percent of people who love you, 30 percent who hate you and 30 percent who couldn't care less." When I heard that, my entire worldview changed.

Suddenly, when someone didn't like me or expressed negativity toward something I was doing, I just said, well, that's from the 30 percent who won't like me no matter what I do or say. Good! Now I can focus on the abundant wealth of support and love I get from my fans and friends who love me and I can love everyone equally. Case closed. Moving on. Thank you very much.

My simple message: You just may be astounded by the sparkly diamond you are hiding beneath the layers of limitational beliefs. You are beautiful. You are raw perfection already; maybe it's time to polish you up, you crazy diamond! I hope to meet you in paradise one day.

Love, Blessings and Namaste,
Dashama

Dashama is exactly right. I've seen it in action repeatedly: no matter who you are, no matter what you do, no matter who your audience is: 30 percent will love it, 30 percent will hate it, and 30 percent won't care. Stick with the people who love you and don't spend a single second on the rest. Life will be better that way.

Which brings me to…

WHAT I LEARNED
FROM SUPERMAN

I jumped off the bed, flew into the air, and landed the wrong way on my foot, breaking it. I was six and there was every indication I was from the planet Krypton, whose sun exploded when I was a baby, leaving me an orphan on a planet filled with people who would never fully understand me

I had a cape on (my Superman blanket). The weak gravity of Earth would not hold me down. Nothing could hold me down. My mother claims she heard the crack of bone from the other side of our suburban house. *Crack!* I landed. It could've happened. She might've heard it.

I had to wear a cast. On the first day of first grade, in a brand-new school, I was "that kid." The one who limped. The one who had a cast. You know, the one you probably would've hung out with because clearly I was destined to be the coolest kid in first grade. At the end of the day I had an itch inside my cast. It was excruciating. And it was raining. The teacher, Mrs. Klecor, wouldn't let us leave to catch our bus at the end of the day unless we could spell our names. I have a bad name for such a task: Altucher. I was sure I was going to miss my bus. I was the last one left. I started to cry. Because I was getting the cast off after school. But not if I couldn't spell my name and I missed my bus.

Almost thirty years later, I'm still Superman.

Or rather, I'm clumsy like Clark Kent. I have glasses. Black hair. I'm often shy in public. People often laugh at me. And, like many people, I have a secret identity that I'm hiding. One that I reveal bit by bit to the Lois Lane closest to me. But nevertheless, if I were to reveal everything I'd end up in jail or a hospital or an institution or more people would hate me than normally do or Claudia would leave me or other people would be badly hurt by those who would take advantage of the real truth. It's my secret identity.

From the age of four to the age of forty-four, I've been reading *Superman*. If I weren't writing this book, I could sit down today and write fifty sample scripts to submit to DC Comics.

Why is the story of Superman so appealing? It's of course the idea that we are all Superman. We are all shy and awkward and IF ONLY PEOPLE KNEW the real us. The one underneath the suit, the glasses—the one who spreads the plain, white shirt apart to reveal the bright colors, the superpowers, the unbelievable intelligence, kindness, the moral and physical strength.

It doesn't have to end. We're taught when we transition from childhood to adulthood to leave behind the stories of our youth. Don't listen to that advice. The stories of our youth, if we all hold onto the hidden gems inside, can help us navigate the world like a superhero. The Choose-Yourself-ers are the new superheroes. The ones who never lost their Kryptonian heritage.

What I Learned from Superman

Start off by realizing you still have a secret identity. Acknowledge it. Wake up every day and say to yourself, "I'm a superhero—what can I do today to save the world?" And there will be answers. And you'll see opportunities. And you'll figure out next steps. You'll figure out how to fly where you are needed. How to lift the car, how to use your X-ray vision to see solutions that nobody thought possible.

If you think about it, Superman actually had no useful powers. We all have the same powers, but we're afraid to admit it. People always say Batman had no powers and Superman did. But it's actually the reverse. Think about it: When would you ever need super strength? Are you really picking up a car anytime soon? No, of course not. Heat vision? What for? I have a microwave. X-ray vision? I can see the most beautiful woman in the world naked anytime I want. All of my neighbors are hideous even with clothes on. And we all know that women in general are sexier with skimpy clothes on than totally naked. And super hearing? I already know what everyone thinks about me. I think I would be horrified to hear them say what I already know they think.

What else? Oh yeah, flying. Where would you fly? And people would see you. And you'd eat flies and run into birds. Ew. Forget it. I'm not flying. I don't even have a driver's license. I'll walk. Or take a train and watch a movie on my iPad. Oh, and bullets don't affect Superman. To be honest, nobody has ever shot at me so this doesn't seem like a useful power to me.

But just knowing I'm Superman, with secret powers, is enough to make me happy. I AM Superman. I'm above the worries of Earthlings. And I believe that with everything inside of me. That's my secret. The secret has power.

The only superpower you really need is the one to constantly cultivate the attitude that forces you to ask, from the minute you wake up, to the minute you fall asleep, "What life can I save today?" It's a practice. Often we forget it. We resist it. Instead of saving lives, we worry about saving ourselves too much. "How will I pay the bills?" "What do I do about my boss saying bad things about me?" And so on.

Instead, superpowers are given to you if all day you try to save at least one life. Try it. Wake up tomorrow and say, "I'm going to save at least one life today." Even helping an old woman across the street counts. Even responding to an e-mail and helping someone make an important decision saves a life. Even reaching out to a distant friend and asking, "How are you doing?" can save their life. You can save a life today. Don't let the sun set without doing that. You are Superman.

Superman is the ultimate yogi. Not because of any flexibility. He's probably not very flexible, actually, because his joints and muscles are super tough. But he follows very well the basic precepts of yoga. He doesn't harm anyone despite his capacity for doing so. He doesn't lie (other than his secret identity, which he holds onto so others aren't harmed). He's never possessive (why be possessive of anything if—like me—he can have anything he wants anytime he wants). He practices "brahmacharya"—a form of self-control—outside of his relationship with the beautiful Lois Lane. Even Napoleon Hill in his classic, *Think and Grow Rich* has an entire chapter on this. Superman also seems to have "santosha" (contentment). He never seems obsessed with grudges from his past. I've never seen him worry about his future. I haven't always been Superman in this respect. But today, NOW is all I care about.

Also, I try to cultivate friendships the way Superman cultivates friendships. He doesn't hang out at the bar with Lex Luthor. Superman is only friends with the Superfriends: the Flash. Black Canary. Wonder Woman. Batman. They all have secret identities. They all see a world totally out of balance. They all have powers they use for good, and which they use to bring balance back to the world. All of my friends are superheroes, too. Each one of my friends has a different power. But they are all amazing powers and I'm blessed when I see those powers in action. And once someone joins the bad guys, they are no longer my friend. I'm busy saving lives. I don't need bad friends.

I'm forty-four now. I no longer need to jump off a bed to prove I can fly. I know I'm going to save a life today. And nobody's going to figure out who I really am. But I will tell you this: I'm Kal-El and I'm from the long-dead planet Krypton.

GANDHI CHOSE HIMSELF TO FREE AN ENTIRE COUNTRY

First, two small stories:

#1: A woman walks with her son many miles and days to come to Gandhi. She is very worried about her son's health because he is eating too much sugar. She comes to Gandhi and says, "Please, sir, can you tell my son to stop eating sugar."

Gandhi looks at her and thinks for a bit and finally says, "Okay, but not today. Bring him back in two weeks."

She's disappointed and takes her son home. Two weeks later she makes the journey again and goes to Gandhi with her son.

Gandhi says to the boy, "You must stop eating sugar. It's very bad for you."

The boy has such respect for Gandhi that he stops and lives a healthy life.

The woman is confused and asks him, "Gandhi, please tell me: Why did you want me to wait two weeks to bring back my son?"

Gandhi said, "Because before I could tell your son to stop eating sugar, I had to stop eating sugar first."

#2: One of Gandhi's financial backers once said, "It's very expensive to keep Gandhi in poverty." Consequently, I suspect the financial backers felt they had some influence on Gandhi. But money means nothing to a spiritual leader.

One time Gandhi said to a group of his backers, "I need to set aside one hour a day to do meditation."

One of the backers said, "Oh no, you can't do that! You are too busy, Gandhi!"

Gandhi said, "Well, then, I now need to set aside two hours a day to do meditation."

Five lessons from this:

A) Nobody can tell you what to do. No matter what they pay you. No matter what obligations you feel you owe them. Every second defines you. Be who you are, not who anyone else is, or who anyone else wants you to be. An entrepreneur, for instance, has investors, customers, partners, employees, and competitors. Everyone wants his input heard. But only you can act to change the world with your ideas.

B) If Gandhi was, in fact too busy, then it meant he was not devoting enough time to his spiritual life. Hence his backer inadvertently convinced him he needed more time to devote to silence and contemplation. It is through silence that sound, activity, and action erupts. It was through nothingness that the Big Bang and all creation erupted. It is only through contemplation that the hidden shades of reality can be seen and right action can be taken. Gandhi knew this, and singlehandedly brought down an empire. It's only through stillness that one can actively create.

C) I don't give any advice on things I don't know about firsthand. Sometimes I find myself in a political conversation and I realize, you know what? I don't actually know anything here. And I give up. Or when someone asks me a question on my Twitter Q&As (held every Thursday between 3:30 and 4:30 p.m. Eastern), I don't say anything unless I have personally experienced or seen the advice I am recommending.

D) Sugar is bad. And since most processed carbs break down into sugar, it's all bad for you if you want to live healthy. Almost every disease out there comes from inflammation and extra weight. The extra weight comes from the sugars that the body breaks down so quickly it forgets to digest. It's no coincidence that, as I mentioned earlier, Ramit Sethi uses flossing as an example in his talks about how to build discipline. It's not just about discipline but health. Flossing is the first line of defense as sugar makes its way through your body.

E) Nothing is more important than the cultivation of yourself. So many people think they will save the world if they defeat "them," where "them" is some evil force that is bringing the world down. But once you divide the world into categories, into an "us" versus "them," then you immediately become a "them" and lose touch with who you really are. And before long you're calling me a fucking douchebag on the Internet.

Society is made up of individuals. The only way to improve society is to come at it from a place of deep, individual satisfaction. The only way to do that is to spend long periods of time just being silent. Find out who the real you is. Ask yourself, "These thoughts that I am thinking, what is generating them?" They are not your thoughts. That is just the biological brain dancing in front of you. Who is the "you" they are dancing in front of? Find that answer, and *then* you can save the world.

The world is made to be filled with strife. Gandhi knew he could only be effective if he identified with the real "me," which was deeper than the body named "Gandhi," who was supposedly saving the world. India is a mess now, no matter what Gandhi did, but Gandhi provided a beacon while he lived.

Both of these stories are about the same thing, even though they seem completely different. Gandhi chose himself. He once said, "You must first be the change you want to see in this World."

Every day I try hard to live by that quote. I hope you can, too.

Nine Things I Learned from Woody Allen

 ▸ ***Try this exercise:*** pretend everyone was sent to this planet to teach you. Famous people, dead people, your neighbors, your relatives, your co-workers. This will give you a strong feeling of humility. And guess what, you will learn from people, you will appreciate them more, and they will actually appreciate you more. Because everyone loves to teach.

Think about what some of the titans of American industry could teach you about failure. Everyone who has ever been a success since the history of mankind began has had to deal with failure. Has had to start from zero—and usually more than once. Whether it was Henry Ford, who went bankrupt with his first car company, or Conrad Hilton, who went bankrupt with Hilton hotels the first time around, or the classic example of Thomas Edison who tried one thousand versions of his lightbulb before he achieved success.

But I'm going to start with a more mundane example. Someone who does whatever he wants, and has built his life, his art, and his career, around doing exactly what he wants: Woody Allen.

I hate Woody Allen. Here's why. Because if you're Jewish and a little neurotic—like Woody Allen—it has become a cliché to describe yourself as "Woody Allen-esque," thinking it will attract women. This happens on dating services all the time. The idea is that you'll attract some waiflike Mia Farrow-ish (or the seventeen-year-old Mariel Hemingway in *Manhattan*) blonde who will love all of your neuroses and want to have sex all the time.

This only happens in Woody Allen movies. And power to him. If Mariel Hemingway wants to have sex with him all the time, then no problem. He wrote and made the movies. He can do whatever the hell he wants in them. It's up to you whether you believe it or not.

And people believe it. Lots of them.

Allen puts out a new movie every year or two. None of them will compete with *Star Wars* or *Harry Potter* in terms of gross dollars. But that doesn't seem to bother his studio. They give him $10 million, his movie makes $20 million, everyone is happy, and he gets to keep doing what he's doing.

So he's built up a substantial body of work that we can learn from. Why learn from him? Because clearly he is a genius, regardless of what other opinions anyone might have of him (and I only know him through his work. I don't know his personal life at all.). It is interesting to see how he, as an artist and creator, has evolved. To see how his idiosyncratic humor has changed, how he twists reality further to stretch our imagination.

He always stands out and stays ahead of the other innovators. And for other people who seek the same, he is worth observing.

Here's some of the things I've learned from him:

1. Failure. One of my earliest memories is having a babysitter while my parents went to a movie. When they got home I asked them what they saw and they described a movie where a man falls asleep and wakes up in the future where a giant nose ruled the world. Woody Allen has been there since the beginning for me. And just the other day, I watched *Midnight in Paris* with Owen Wilson (who, despite looking very un-Woody Allen-esque, plays the virtual "Woody Allen" role very well). The movie explores the history of art and how no art form exists by itself but is always influenced by generation after generation of artists before it, dating back hundreds if not thousands of years. It's one of his best.

But some of his movies are just awful. He admits it. In a 1976 interview in *Rolling Stone*, he said, "I would like to fail a little for the public...What I want to do is go onto some areas that I'm insecure about and not so good at."

He elaborates further. He admits he could be like the Marx Brothers and make the same comic film every year. But he didn't want to do it. It was important for him to evolve. To risk failure. To risk failure in front of everyone. And his movies did that, going from the early slapstick humor of *Sleeper* to the darker *Crimes and Misdemeanors* and *Match Point*.

Woody Allen has failed spectacularly, in every way we can imagine—personally, professionally, etc. And yet he's always pushing forward, trying to surprise us again and again, and largely succeeding rather than giving up.

2. Prophetic. In a 1977 *Washington Post* interview he said, "We're probably living at the end of an era. I think it's only a matter of time until home viewing is as easy and economical as desirable." In the past three days I've watched three Woody Allen movies on my iPad. I don't know if technology changed the way he made his movies. But it's clear he never got himself stuck in one particular form or style that would eventually fail to cater to the tastes of the average audience. To be creative and stand out in today's world, you must always be diversifying the artistic experience you put out.

3. Flexible. We admire the Choose-Yourself-ers who quickly recognize mistakes and then transition their business accordingly (the catchphrase lately is that these entrepreneurs know how to "pivot"). Allen typically starts off with a broad outline, a sort of script, but it changes throughout the movie. In a 1978 interview with Ira Halberstadt he says, "To me a film grows organically. I write the script and then it changes organically. I see people come in and then I decide…it changes here. It changes if Keaton doesn't want to do these lines and I don't want to do these—we shift around. It changes for a million reasons."

The entrepreneur, the entre-ployee. In general, all relationships in general shift and change. You set out in life wanting certain things—the college degree, the house with the white fence, the promotions, the family—but things become different. You have to adapt and be flexible.

4. Productivity. To put out a movie every year or so, plus plays, magazine stories, and books, you would think Woody Allen works around the clock. In a 1980 interview, "If you work only three to five hours a day you become very productive. It's the steadiness of it that counts. Getting to the typewriter every day is what makes productivity."

He states later in the interview that when he was younger he liked to get things out in one impulsive burst but he learned that was a "bad habit," and that he likes to wake up early, do his work, and then set it aside for the next day.

Probably the most productive schedule is to wake up early—do your work before people start showing up at your doorstep, on your phone, in your inbox, etc., and leave off at the point right when you are most excited to continue. Then you know it will be easy to start off the next day.

I read in a recent interview that it takes Allen a month to write a comedy and three months to write a drama. On three to five hours a day, it shows me he writes *every day*, he's consistent, and he doesn't waste time with distractions (going to parties, staying out late).

5. Avoid outside stimulus. These days, I make a huge mistake every day. I start off with the loop: e-mail, Twitter, Facebook, my Amazon rank, my blog stats, my blog comments. Claudia asks me, "Did you finish the loop yet?" And I think it will only take a few seconds but it actually takes about twenty minutes. I probably do it ten times a day. That's two hundred minutes! Three hours and twenty minutes! Ugh.

Do you know where Allen was sitting when he won an Oscar for *Annie Hall*? In Michael's Pub in Manhattan, playing his weekly jazz clarinet gig. Why get on a plane (eight hours, door to door), and go to a party where he would feel uncomfortable, to win an award he probably didn't care much about (although it magnified his prestige in Hollywood, the city that paid his bills)?

In a 1982 interview with the *Washington Post* he said, "I probably would not have watched anyway," just to see everyone he knows hunched down in the audience waiting for hours to see who would win. Besides, he had "a very nice time" at Michael's. For Allen, his pleasure came first, rather than the anxious watching and waiting.

Then he went home. He went out the back way of Michael's to skip all the photographers out front and was home by midnight for his "milk and cookies." Then, he went to sleep. And TOOK THE PHONE OFF THE HOOK. Who even does that now? In an age where we (or, I should say, "I") literally sleep with the iPad and phone in bed. He took the phone off the hook on Oscar night and went to sleep. In the morning, he made his coffee and toast, got the *New York Times*, and only then finally opened it up to the entertainment section, where he saw he'd won the Oscar. Amazing. He didn't even care when no one was looking. It's in this way that he keeps his productivity (compared with the lack of productivity many of us suffer now because of the constant influx of outside social stimulants) at a very high point.

6. Imperfection. Allen has said many times that none of his films were exactly what he wanted. That they were constantly imperfect. It's almost like he's the imperfect perfectionist. He wants things just right, and he tries very hard to get them that way. But he knows it will never happen.

That said, he doesn't give up. He said in 1986, "We go out and shoot…again…and again…and again, if necessary. And even at that rate, all the pictures come up imperfect. Even at that meticulous rate of shooting them over and over again, they still come out flawed. None of them is close to being perfect." Ultimately, he says, all his movies prove to be "great disappointments."

And yet, knowing that he will always experience the same thing, he goes out, stretches the boundaries of where he's comfortable in failing, and does it again. And again. Knowing nothing he will do will be the masterpiece he initially conceived.

Nothing comes out exactly how we want it. But we have to learn to roll with it and move to the next work.

7. Confidence. I watched *Husbands and Wives* the other day. It wasn't a funny movie. It wasn't a pretty movie. I watched it with Claudia and by the end we were both thinking, Ugh, I hope that doesn't happen to us in ten years. The movie itself was jarring. Instead of being shot traditionally it was shot with a hand-held camera. It was edited with lots of jump-cuts, where you're looking at a character and suddenly she's an inch over because some small piece of film was cut out. The editing itself became part of the jolting and jarring in the story. It was as if the story was not just being told with the acting and the writing but with the way it was shot and edited.

It reminded me of something Kurt Vonnegut, considered an experimental writer in his own right, once said: "To be experimental, first you have to know how to use all the rules of grammar. You have to be an expert first in tradition." It also reminds me of Andy Warhol, who was a highly paid, very straightforward, commercial artist, before he went experimental and started the pop art phenomenon.

In a 1994 interview, Allen said about *Husbands and Wives* (note: *Husbands and Wives* was his twentieth movie): "Confidence that comes with experience enables you to do many things that you wouldn't have done in earlier films. You tend to become bolder…you let your instincts operate more freely and you don't worry about the niceties."

In other words: master the form you want to operate in, get experience, be willing to be imperfect, and then develop the confidence to play within that form, to develop your own style. You see this in Kurt Vonnegut, too, as he transformed from the more traditional *Player Piano* in the early '50s to *Slaughterhouse-Five* in 1969, a novel about World War II that includes aliens who can time travel.

8. Showing up. As Allen famously stated, 80 percent of success is "showing up." Nothing more really needs to be added there except it might be changed to "Ninety-nine percent of success for the entrepreneur is showing up." What do you have to show up for? You have to find the investors, you have to manage development, you have to find the first customers, *You* have to find the buyers. They don't show up at your door. *You show up* at their door. Otherwise your business will just not work out. Let's take Microsoft as one example among many. Bill Gates tracked down the guy in New Mexico to build BASIC. Bill Gates put himself in the middle when IBM wanted to license an operating system. He just kept showing up while everyone else was skiing.

9. The medium becomes the message. I mentioned this in the point above but it deserves further elaboration. The jump-cutting, the handheld camera, every aspect of *Husbands and Wives* became woven in with the story. Allen said, "I wanted it to be more dissonant, because the internal emotional and mental states of the characters are more dissonant. I wanted the audience to feel there was a jagged and nervous feeling." In this he shows not only his own evolution as a filmmaker but what he's borrowed from the artists before him—not only Godard and Bergman, who did their own experimentations, but musicians like Profokiev, where the dissonance itself is so tightly wound with the music that it becomes a part of the music, as opposed to just the notes being played. This is underlined at a very high level in Allen's latest movie, *Midnight in Paris*, when Owen Wilson, the main character, pinpoints the roots of his own art by going back further and further in time.

My takeaway? Study the history of the form you want to master. Study every nuance. If you want to write, read not only all of your contemporaries, but the influences of those contemporaries, and their influences. Additionally, draw inspiration from other art forms. From music, art, and there again, go back to the influences of your inspirations, and go back to their influences, and so on. The facets that resonate with time, even if it's hundreds of years old, will resonate with your work as well. It's like a law of the universe.

In today's day and age, we want to transform decades of work into years or even months. Allen built up his career over five decades and kept at it persistently, even when scandal, or a bad movie, or a bad article, would cast gloom over his entire trajectory. But he shrugged it off.

So what can we learn from Woody Allen?

- Wake up early.
- Avoid distractions.
- Work three to five hours a day and then enjoy the rest of the day.
- Be as perfectionist as you can, knowing that imperfection will still rule.
- Have the confidence to be magical and stretch the boundaries of your medium.

- Combine the tools of the medium itself with the message you want to convey.
- Don't get stuck in the same rut—move forward, experiment, but with the confidence built up over experience.
- Change the rules but learn them first.

The same can be said for any successful Choose-Yourself-er. Or for people who are successful in any aspect of life. Is Woody Allen a happy man? Who knows? But he's done what he set out to do. He's made movies. He's told stories. He's lived the dream, even when it bordered on nightmare. We can only be so lucky.

COMPETENCE AND THE BEATLES' LAST CONCERT

On January 30, 1969 the Beatles hated each other, and they were sick of working on their album *Let It Be* inside of their cramped studios. On a whim, they took all their equipment and moved it five floors up to the roof, in the middle of winter. Then they performed for about a half hour. They had last performed live more than two years earlier. It was their last "concert" ever. They broke up shortly afterward and never performed together again.

I say it was a "concert" because people in the blocks around them quickly began to realize what was happening. People couldn't believe it. You see office workers climbing out of windows and down ladders to get a better view. Women running up and down the streets to try and see better. An older man with a pipe climbing up a fire escape to stand on a rooftop and watch. After about ten minutes, the streets were crowded with people staring up at the roof of the building where the music was coming from. People on the ground couldn't see the band but they knew it was them. The effect of the Beatles singing live shut down London for a half hour.

About halfway through, so-called reality started to hit some of the passersby. One guy said, "It's a bit of an imposition to absolutely disrupt all of the business in this area." We'll never know the name of that guy. We'll never know what he was working on in January 1969 that was so important. Or what any of the "business" in that area was that winter afternoon. But forty-three years later we still watch the video. We still listen to the songs.

A couple of things I find interesting about this video:

A) The members of the group hated each other. At this point the Beatles were basically over. The album was originally called *Get Back* after one of the songs in it. But they couldn't "get back" together and ultimately it was called *Let It Be*. It was their last released album. You can blame it on anything: Yoko, Linda, creative conflicts, Phil Spector, Brian Epstein's death, on and on. But whatever the real "reason(s)," they hated each other despite the mega success they had created together.

B) You can see on their faces as they get to the roof: they were never going to perform again. Ringo looks sad. George Harrison looks particularly upset. In fact, a few weeks earlier he and John Lennon had gotten into a fistfight and Harrison had run out and said he was "quitting." "See you in the clubs," he said as he left. The band debated replacing him with Eric Clapton but Harrison came back. McCartney had the wherewithal to say that the Beatles wouldn't be the Beatles without the four members.

C) Harrison hated the fact that Lennon was growing more and more detached from the band and doing his own thing. Lennon hated Harrison's and McCartney's music writing. (Lennon, after the album came out, said of "The Long and Winding Road" and producer Phil Spector's treatment of it: "He was given the shit-tiest load of badly recorded shit with a lousy feeling to it ever, and he made something of it.") In other words, they hated each other. And they didn't hold back. They just simply did not want to work with each other anymore despite the years of creative and financial success. George Harrison joined the Beatles when he was fourteen years old. They had grown up together.

D) The second song they sing in the video, "Don't Let Me Down," is poignant. It was originally written by John Lennon for Yoko. Despite his success, Lennon was terrified of being let down by Yoko. Despite our attempts to climb away from the worst fears of our childhood, success only magnifies those fears. We're like birds trying to climb a tree to reach for the freedom of the blue sky. Only when we learn how to fly can we truly be free. For Lennon, being let down as a kid or young adult exploded into a plea not only to one woman but to millions of eventual listeners.

It feels like he's not just singing it to her. He's singing it to the Beatles, who he felt let down by. He's singing it out there to the air, to the blocks of people staring out their windows at him. He's singing to London. He's pleading to his future, where he would be creatively on his own—"Don't Let Me Down." And, prophetically, the world let him down in the worst way on December 8, 1980. The song never made it to the final, released album. I like the original shot in the video, of Lennon and McCartney singing it together, with Ringo in the middle in the background. The three were barely speaking to each other at that point. They had all let each other down. And yet that wouldn't prevent them from creating beautiful music.

E) Competence. Despite all the troubles. Despite their contempt for each other's musical abilities. Despite the fragmented legal and emotional fallouts that were quickly cascading them toward the band's demise, they went up on that stage and PERFORMED. I've listened to the video a hundred times. Paul opens his mouth and the music begins and doesn't stop for twenty minutes. It's beautiful. Competent people move forward and do what they do. I hope in my life I can be as good at any one thing as the four of them were at what they did that day, but I doubt it will happen.

And finally, "beginner's mind."

At the end of the video, with the police now getting into the action and telling them to shut it down because of noise complaints, they finish with the song "Get Back" again. Paul McCartney riffs in the middle of the song, "You've been playing on the roofs again, and you know your Momma doesn't like it, she's gonna have you arrested!"

And when they finally put their instruments down, John Lennon only half sarcastically says (the last line the Beatles ever say to an audience), "On behalf of the group and ourselves, I hope we pass the audition."

A creator can't ever rest. No matter what you do, no matter what your creation is. Every moment is the audition. Every time you create is a chance to go on the roof and do something new, in a way that hasn't been done before, in a way that is potentially disruptive, playful, unique, and vulnerable. People will hate you, people will love you, people will climb on the rooftops to see you before the police arrest you. The Beatles passed the audition that one last time. Now it's our turn.

WHAT TO DO WHEN
YOU ARE REJECTED

Everyone around the table had been brutally rejected hundreds of times. I was at a dinner with a bunch of authors who had gone the self-publishing route via Amazon. All of them had chosen themselves. And all of them, except for me, were fiction writers who had sold more than one hundred thousand copies or more of their various novels. The guy sitting across from me had just sold the movie rights to his latest science fiction series. Another woman was working on the sequel to her "young adult paranormal" series. Another guy had sold more than five hundred thousand copies of his various thrillers. The guy sitting next to me had been very successful at his "children's chapter books" series, *Sweet Farts*.

All of them had one thing in common. While pursuing the career of their dreams they had all been rejected. Some of them hundreds of times. All of them were either on the verge of writing full-time for a living or had already made the leap. Every one of them was smiling.

How many would've been smiling if they had given up after the thirty-ninth rejection and didn't go for that fortieth? Or didn't go for it that moment when they decided, I'm going to take control of the creative process and not stop where the gatekeepers tell me to stop.

SO MANY TIMES I'VE BEEN STOPPED BY THE GATEKEEPERS. At a job, for instance, where my boss said, "Stop working on this and focus on your main job." Or when I was trying to sell a TV show and there were only one or two decision makers and they all blocked my path for political reasons. Or I wanted to sell a company and there were only a few decision makers who could make or break what I thought then was my entire life. The stark fear I had whenever I spoke to them, knowing they had this enormous power over me, and foolishly thinking that I had nothing to offer them.

Every day, in all aspects of our lives, we are rejected. Rejection is probably the most powerful force in our lives. Think back on the times you've been rejected and how your response to it changed your life completely. There are three basic responses to rejection that I've seen (in just the past few days I've seen examples of all of these).

"I suck. I can't do this. I give up."

"They are stupid. I'm going to keep pushing forward."

"Hmm, what can I do differently? What can I learn from this rejection?"

Obviously I'm going to ignore the first two. It could be the case that you need to give up. Or it could be the case that you should do nothing to improve and you just push forward, but that should never be the gut response (although, again, I've seen it as the gut response several times from various people in just the past few days/months/years/myself/etc.).

So how can you take rejection and use it to push forward?

IMPROVE. You wanted that ONE job, that ONE scholarship, that TV show, that book, to sell your company, to sell your product, whatever. And they said, no. Take a hard look at the product. Can you improve your offering? Can you take a step back and improve what you are doing? Maybe you can and maybe you can't. But brainstorm first. What are the ten things you can do to improve what you are doing?

One time I tried to sell a company that I had started. The company didn't have enough clients or enough revenues. And I was a bit inconsistent about the services we were offering that made us unique. There were about ten different areas I needed to improve and gradually I improved them all and sold the company a year later.

EXPAND THE UNIVERSE OF DECISION MAKERS. Until the past two or three years, if you wanted to sell a novel there were basically five to ten decision makers. Every year almost twenty thousand people would submit novels to these decision makers (the major publishing houses) and most would get rejected. Who would reject you? Interns and assistants who had just graduated college with a degree in comparative literature, who barely even looked at what you wrote.

Now you can self-publish via Amazon (or through this book's publisher, Lioncrest), and it's a great process. You just chose yourself but, more important, the readers become your decision makers. The universe of millions of readers will now help you make your next decisions on how to improve, how to gain more power over your creative process, and finally, how to secure power over your entire life.

THIS IS THE CHOOSE YOURSELF ERA. When I was visiting with Amazon, I was amazed at what a revolution was going on. It's not about an extra device. It's about how for the first time since Gutenberg there's an actual revolution in how you can communicate with the masses. In every way, you can choose yourself now to succeed, to improve, to communicate, to extend your reach to the individuals who need your message. Don't give up on this opportunity. In fact, "rejection" might be what forces you into it, as it did for the twenty or so authors I met last week.

And it's not just novels. It's everything. Can you widen the audience for your product? Online dating has expanded the decision makers in your relationship life. And YouTube has greatly expanded the universe of tastemakers who will define your fate. I hate to say it, but Justin Bieber uploading YouTube videos of himself (and now exceeding 2 billion video views) greatly increased his chances of success instead of trying to go the same route as everyone else—through the traditional five to ten record labels deciding your fate. All respect to the kid, who chose himself and made it work.

IMPROVE YOUR APPROACH. You keep getting rejected in bars? Find a different place, where the odds aren't stacked against you. Nobody responding to your networking e-mails for "Ten minutes of your time please?" Then offer something. Give something for free so people immediately see value in your approach immediately. You keep cold-calling customers and they hang up? Find a different way to get distribution.

CHANGE UP, DON'T GIVE UP. I was the guy who "gave up" on the thirty-ninth try when trying to sell a novel I had written. Sometimes the odds are just too stacked against you. Maybe it would've worked on the fortieth try. I don't know. But I'm glad I gave up; I "changed up" instead. Rather than focusing on fiction as the only creative medium, I started looking at both TV and the brand-new World Wide Web as creative media. Which led to a job at HBO. Which led to my first company focusing on building content-heavy websites for entertainment companies.

I didn't give up on being creative. I expanded the power of my creativity by not limiting myself to one domain, and vowing to return to book-writing later, ultimately to fiction-writing. Maybe I'll do it, maybe I won't. But the "Change Up" certainly released me creatively, and I was able to use it to build both my financial life and creative life. We'll see if it ever comes full circle.

IMPROVE YOUR AUTHENTICITY. Social media can also be called "Individual media" as opposed to "Group Media." Instead of a large group broadcasting your effort, you can build up your own presence by establishing your Facebook platform, your Twitter presence, your LinkedIn, Quora, Pinterest, blogging, Amazon, SlideShare, Scribd, reddit, etc., presence. All of these channels are used to create authenticity for your offering. Each follower, fan, etc., you are personally able to sway over to your side of the world continues to establish your authenticity, regardless of who is "rejecting" you. This is how you choose yourself and build your own platform rather than relying on the whims of a meager few.

ASK FOR ADVICE. Someone rejected you? Poor baby! Now, after your mourning is over, ask why. You're going to be rejected all your life. In every way. It never hurts to understand why. Sometimes they will even tell you and, in those cases, it's a guarantee that you will remember.

DANCE WITH FAILURE. You just got rejected? How did you deal with it? Did you cry? Did you give up? Did you think to yourself, Why do I ALWAYS fail? Did you think to yourself, Those guys are STUPID for rejecting me? Understand your reaction to failure. What can you do to improve it?

The other day I read that 76 percent of the universe is comprised of "dark energy." In other words, we have zero clues as to what it is. Another 20 percent is "dark matter," i.e., matter that we have no clue about. Only 4 percent of the universe is actually made up of matter we understand. In other words, after Newton, Einstein, Heisenberg, and two thousand years of collective exploration of the universe and all its elements, we've basically failed. In fact, the more knowledge we get, the more we realize how badly we are failing. We used to think we had it down. But now even the Big Bang theory is in serious question. We just suck at understanding the world around us.

Do physicists cry themselves to sleep every night because they have failed so badly? Of course not. This failure has only given them opportunity to discover more. It's opened up vast landscapes of potential understanding that can actually help us understand what the universe is, and in that understanding, help us understand who we are.

Not every failure is an opportunity. But figure it out. Look at the times you failed. How many, in retrospect, were opportunities. About two years ago, I had a billionaire who wanted to give me about $50 million to start a fund. A mutual friend of ours blocked it for some reason I still don't know. At the time I was upset.

Now I'm grateful. I've done so many things since then that I'm very happy I did and I never would've done if I was busy running a fund. Thank god I got rejected! I never would've written this book, for instance.

ACKNOWLEDGMENT OF THE PROCESS: The NORMAL thing is to be rejected. To get rejected by jobs, your kids, friends, family members, relationships, businesses, publishers, everyone. As Dashama put it in her e-mail to me (see "The Curious Case of the Sexy Image"): a third will like you, a third will hate you, a third won't care...no matter what you do.

It's actually ABNORMAL to "get close" to not being rejected. It's even more abnormal to be "accepted" or to "succeed" in some conventional sense. So acknowledge that it's perfectly normal to feel rejected over something. And it's perfectly normal to fear it for the future. In fact, to do otherwise would be to reject reality.

But also acknowledge the successes. The things that occur that are abnormal. The things you do to improve. The things you learn on the road to choosing yourself.

Don't fall back into a story ("I always get rejected") that is more fairy tale than reality.

STAY IN TOUCH. It's hard for me to not burn bridges. I tend to do it too much. But I've found great success when I've not fallen into the bridge-burning pattern I often succumb to.

Example: I once tried to sell an early company I started to Omnicom, the big ad agency. I met with the woman who made these decisions for Omnicom. She felt we weren't ready yet.

Every month I sent her an update: new clients, new sales numbers, number of employees. I also offered to help any of the agencies that Omnicom had. One time I called her on behalf of one of my clients to see if she could recommend any agencies within the Omnicom family to help one of my clients. In other words, I offered her real value.

After about a year of me doing this every month, she rallied three of the agencies within Omnicom to come over and check out my company. All three made offers. Did I accept any? No, but I was able to leverage those offers into a better offer from someone who came completely out of the blue.

I hate the phrase *Life is too short*. Sometimes it feels very long to me. But it's certainly too short to spend any time on hard feelings. Everyone is just trying to get by. Both the rejected and the rejecters. Nobody is free from this. So let's all keep in touch. It'll be a tiny bit easier to make it to the finish line.

Surviving Failure

Perhaps the best thing that happened to me in 2012 was I said no to being run over by a tank in Santiago, Chile. "You won't get hurt," said Mattias, "trust me, there's enough space underneath the tank." The invitation was at the request of the president of Chile, who earlier that year had put out a press release saying his net worth had increased by $200 million since he had become president. This was capitalism at work, and he had invited me down to be an eyewitness to it.

Someone wrote me that they were very upset because a deal they had been working on all year had not worked out. "How do you get past this?" he asked. Many times I get asked that. "How do I get past this bad thing that happened to me?" A relationship, a deal, an illness, an insult. And I deal with this question myself. Lots of bad things happen.

"How do you get past this?" Diversification is everything. You get past "this" by having lots of "that"s.

But on top of everything there's one more thing. **Being like a child.** Fittingly, I am finishing this book on the last night of 2012. Last night my daughter woke me up and she was crying.

"I forgot to do my homework today!" she said. "That's okay, honey, we'll do it tomorrow." "But then New Year's Eve Day is ruined," she said. "It's a holiday!" "Okay, we'll do it the next day," I told her, trying to calm her down so I could get back to sleep. "But New Year's Day is a holiday!" and she was crying and I had run out of days.

Like we all will at some point. We'll run out of days. And a child will cry and miss us. And eventually another child will cry and miss them when they are all grown up and the life is withered out of them.

Diversification is one thing, but a child forgets. January 2 will happen and my daughter won't care what day it was that she got her homework done. January 3 will happen and my daughter won't even remember if she had homework this past weekend, and January 4 will happen and my daughter won't even remember any of the things she learned in her homework. January 5 will happen, though, and I'll still remember all the bad things that happened to me personally in 2012. Forget about failing at just one deal. **In 2012 I had:**

- Three funds I tried to start and couldn't get off the ground.
- I tried to get someone to buy $1 billion worth of FB stock (before it went public) and failed
- I tried to get someone to sell $300,000 worth of Twitter stock and failed
- I tried to get a $1 billion dollar JV on an oil deal done
- I tried to buy 1 million barrels of oil for someone and failed
- three companies I invested in, I had to write off as zeros

- I'm waiting to hear today if a company I invested in gets funding or if they will depend on me to avoid going broke by the end of today.
- I sold a house I never lived in, and lost $800,000 on it. Just glad to get rid of it now.
- My oldest became a teenager (which turns out to be a much bigger loss for me than I realized it would be. I will never have those years back.).
- My mother accused me of killing my father and will no longer speak to me.
- Both my sisters no longer speak to me.
- I get nonstop hate mail. I got one today saying I was "too Jewish," whatever that means. And over the weekend I got one from a Jewish guy saying I was a disgrace to Jews. So I don't win either way.
- I got results back from testing my DNA. I have double the risk of everyone else of getting Alzheimer's. Ditto for Parkinson's. I told a friend I was going to write *The APo4E Diet* (Apo4e being the gene or chromosome or whatever for Alzheimer's). She wrote back it would be a bestseller because everyone would forget if they had bought it already.

I was six when I got together one of those rockets that you fill up with water and then it shoots into the air, spraying water everywhere. It goes up a hundred feet. "Will it go into space?" I asked my dad. "Maybe," he said. And why not? I was six, and anything could happen.

I was six when I designed a pair of glasses that could see backward. I drew it and showed it to my grandparents. "You drew this?" said my grandpa, and right then I was pleased with my invention. I was six when I believed not only in Jesus but in Zeus and Hermes and Thor and Superman, and my only wish was to be a superhero when I grew up.

When you're a kid, everything has a question mark at the end of it. Only later do they turn into periods. Or even exclamation points. "Will I get over this?" becomes "It's too late." Becomes "I can't get over this!"

My only hope for my future is I learn to dot the landscape of my life once more with question marks instead of periods. To turn judgments into queries. To turn "this" into "that?" To make every problem a maze. To be like a six-year-old. The next time the president of Chile wants me to get run over by a tank I might say yes. Or I might ride away on my spaceship and French-kiss the angel on the moon. "Lips are beautiful," I might say, before finally falling back to Earth.

Take Over the World

Okay.

It's over.

That whole "job" thing. The corporate safety net that the Industrial Revolution created. We thought we were "safe." That we didn't have to make it on our own anymore. That big corporations would take care of us once we paid our dues with a college education.

Well, that was a myth. I can't say it was a lie, because we all truly believed it. From the top down, we wanted to make it happen. But society isn't so simple. You can't break apart spirit from science, arts from finance, or jobs from innovation, and expect the results to be clean and neat. They aren't. And the shift has already happened. The earth has split apart.

Some will fall into the abyss created when the earth quakes. Some will not be able to master the tools of keeping healthy and building the platform of self-sufficiency that is necessary to choose yourself.

But many will. I hope the readers of this book will.

The key is not different from any other time in history. But it's more immediate now if we want not only to survive but to flourish.

It is, of course, to help ourselves. Help ourselves to health. Give ourselves more choices instead of being reliant on others. And then creating wealth for ourselves. Financial wealth, emotional wealth, and spiritual wealth.

One way to think about it is with the image of the circle:

I want you to take out a pen and a piece of paper and do something for me.

Draw a little circle. Put what you do in that circle. If you're a secretary, put "secretary." If you're an artist, put "artist." If you are a mother, put "mother." Put the thing that is central to your life. If you are unsure what is central to your life, put your job title. If you don't have a job title, put what title you would like to be central to your life.

Draw a circle around that. Draw lines dividing up the second circle into compartments. Like apartments in a space station. Write down the names of the people who are affected by your first circle. Maybe you help them do better jobs. Maybe you're a doctor and they are your patients. Maybe you are a secretary and they are your colleagues, your bosses, your family whom you provide for, your relatives who listen to you, your friends who rely on you. If you are a blogger, they are your readers.

Draw a circle around that one. Draw the lines again. Who lives in these compartments? The people who are affected by the people you affect. For instance, the children of your friends. The friends of your children. The people related to your employees. Or your employers. This would be in the third circle.

Next circle: what your center circle can turn into. A blog can turn into a book, or a show, or a consulting service, or a novel, or who knows? Keep thinking of it. A janitor can rise up to be CEO of a company. Make your brain sweat. A doctor's job can turn into a business, a book, advice, a class, a mission. A secretary can turn into a boss, a company. What does your center circle evolve into if you stick with it over time?

Draw one more circle: the people you would like to affect. Maybe you would like to affect Barack Obama. Or a movie producer. Or a book publisher. Or the CEO of your company. Or all the venture capitalists in the world. Put them there. Why not? We're just drawing. We're just playing.

It's not impossible. For instance, Oprah can read my blog. Maybe she has already. Or maybe the relative of an initial reader shows Gayle King my blog or my books, who shows Oprah. It's possible.

And then finally one more circle. This circle has everyone in the world in it. Because of Oprah or Barack or a book publisher or if all the venture capitalists in the world are strongly affected by your work then eventually the entire world, in some small way, the indent in a paragraph in the tale of our history, will be changed.

Maybe you can't draw these circles. Maybe you think your work, or your love, or your friendship, or your charitable efforts, or whatever you consider your "center" today (just today, we only care about today) doesn't affect anyone else. Or if it does, maybe you feel the effect stops there. Or even if the effect moves on, spreading like a disease, it disappears over distance or over time, until finally its impact on the world is negligible. Nil. Nothing.

That's okay. Start over. Tweak something. Maybe you aren't a secretary or a doctor. Maybe deep down you are an artist. Maybe you're a mother. Or a father. And the impact is further reaching than you thought. Do the circles over. Do it over until you can draw that outer circle and affect the entire world. Throw out the old people. Draw more circles.

When we were kids and took a bad test, everyone would yell, "I want a redo!" We're not in school. We're in life. You have your redo. Again and again. Draw the circles again. Keep drawing them until you finally have that outer circle. The circle of possibility. The one where the entire world changes because you exist.

Redo!

Too many people, in the rush of their lives, stop at just the second circle, the ones they immediately impact. They might even stop before that. Maybe they just wonder how their first circle impacts only themselves. Don't stop. Push yourself outward. See the web you spin. See how the world is caught in that web. Push yourself until that web is spun all around, circles within circles within circles. This is not about making the most money, or having the most impact. This is about being connected with who you are. This is about seeing how far your potential truly can unravel, simply because you are human.

And start connecting the inner circles with the outer circles in deeper and deeper ways. Eventually the lines between the circles go away. It's one big circle. You're in the middle. You're doing the daily practice. You're choosing yourself. You're the source. And your light and choices are now affecting everyone.

Are you better off? Yes. We're all better off. Thank you.

TESTIMONIALS

I'm always grateful to get e-mails or see tweets where people mention the help they have received from some of these ideas. When you share an idea that worked for you, all you ever really know is this: it worked for you.

So it's nice when people say it worked for them also. That your experiences are translatable into other lives. And that your way of expressing them was an effective way of communicating those experiences.

These are just a few of the testimonials I've gotten. I took a one day snapshot of e-mails and tweets I received.

Again, I'm very grateful to receive them and others, and I hope people always stay in touch with me to let me know how things are going.

Andrew Ferri @Andrew_Ferri

"Been doing my daily practice so long I got it on auto-pilot. Now when people ask me how'd I get so awesome I just say, "Ever heard of @jaltucher?""

Scott Balster @scottbalster

"@jaltucher. WHEN you come to CO I am building u a hand-crafted throne & carrying you on my back to a slice of heaven."

Carrie Armstrong @CarrieArmstrng

"Ah Colonel Altucher—your blog is finger lickin good."

jackyism @jackyism

"@jaltucher all I can say is wow and thank you."

Doctor Coke @AmielCocco

"@jaltucher Loved your article '10 reasons why 2013...' It gave me strength to finally start my own business."

"Your articles have served for a noble, wonderful purpose in my life. I get fresh perspectives every time I read them." (Cesar Trujillo)

"You've perfected the art of storytelling." (Joe Choi)

"In so many ways, what you are doing is revolutionary. But don't think about that too much or it could 'jinx' it. Just keep perfecting yourself." (James Kostohryz)

"You are a beacon of honesty, James. Every time I read your posts, I see things in a different light." (Ashish Hablani)

"I found I was able to smile thru one of my toughest workdays in 16 years. @jaltucher, your blog got me started on the way to this. Thanks." (Cristy Skram, @UCAGWUW)

"James, just wanted to let you know you are one of my biggest inspirations. I needed to send a personal thank you through here." (Vincent Nguyen, @SelfStairway)

Testimonials

"I don't expect you to remember me, don't feel like you have to respond to this please. 2 years ago, you quite literally saved my life.

I was in rough shape, had lost my dream job, my wife and I were on the edge, I had to take a crap job, the list went on.

I had found your site, I sent you an e-mail and you had actually taken the time to respond. I've never forgotten that.

Things got worse but I fought like hell, in large part because of your advice, and slowly started to pick myself up off the ground.

Now, things are getting better. I got a better full time job, my wife and I have had a better relationship, my kids are happy and live well and I'm working my butt off to realize a few dreams.

James, man, I know you must hear this so often but you changed my life. Thank you, thank you for taking the time two years ago, thank you for being who you are."

—Anon

Please send me your e-mails at altucher@gmail.com

JAMES ALTUCHER

JAMES ALTUCHER is a successful entrepreneur, chess master, investor and writer. He has started and run more than 20 companies, and sold several of those businesses for large exits. He has also run venture capital funds, hedge funds, angel funds, and currently sits on the boards of several companies. His writing has appeared in most major national media outlets (*Wall Street Journal*, ABC, *Financial Times*, Tech Crunch, *Forbes*, CNBC, etc). His blog has attracted more than 10 million readers since its launch in 2010. This is his 11th book.

54670556R00153

Made in the USA
Lexington, KY
24 August 2016